# Straightedge Youth

16 30

**Complexity and Contradictions of a Subculture**

# Robert T. Wood

RESS

First Edition 2006

06   07   08   09   10   11         6   5   4   3   2   1

The paper used in this publication meets the minimum requirements of American National Standard for Information Sciences—Permanence of Paper for Printed Library Materials, ANSI Z39.48–1984.∞™

Parts of chapter 2 first appeared in Robert T. Wood, " 'Nailed to the X': A Lyrical History of the Straightedge Youth Subculture," *Journal of Youth Studies* 2 (1999): 133–51.

Parts of chapter 3 first appeared in Robert T. Wood, "Straightedge Youth: Observations on the Complexity of Subcultural Identity," *Journal of Youth Studies* 6, no. 1 (2003): 33–52.

Parts of chapter 6 first appeared in Robert T. Wood, "Threat Transcendence, Ideological Articulation, and Frame of Reference Reconstruction: Preliminary Concepts for a Theory of Subcultural Schism," *Deviant Behavior* 21, no. 1 (2000): 23–45.

**Library of Congress Cataloging-in-Publication Data**
Wood, Robert T., 1972–
Straightedge youth : complexity and contradictions of a subculture / Robert T.
Wood.—1st ed.
p. cm.
Includes bibliographical references and index.
ISBN 0–8156–3127–8 (hardcover : alk. paper)
1. Youth—United States. 2. Straight-edge culture—United States. 3. Subculture—
United States. 4. Straight-edge (Music)—United States. I. Title.
HQ796.W636 2006
306'.1097309045—dc22                 2006020322

Being true is following the basic, quote unquote, rules of not drinking, not smoking, not doing drugs, and no promiscuous sexual activity. Don't smoke, don't drink, don't fuck. Those are the rules. If you don't want to follow the rules, then unclaim.

> —**A straightedger,** commenting on what it means to be straightedge

I don't like it when people view it as a set of rules. You know, where you have to do A, B, and C. I don't think that's what it's all about. It's not like it comes with a manual that tells you, "Okay, here's the steps."

> —**A straightedger,** commenting on what it means to be straightedge

**Robert T. Wood** is an associate professor of sociology at the University of Lethbridge in Alberta, Canada. After earning a B.A. Honors degree from the University of Alberta, he went on to earn an M.A. from the University of Toronto and a Ph.D. from the University of Alberta. Dr. Wood's research interests are varied, spanning theories of criminology, the sociocultural aspects of problem gambling, and the dynamics of contemporary youth subcultures. He has contributed articles on youth subculture to *Deviant Behavior, Youth and Society,* and the *Journal of Youth Studies.*

# Contents

# Acknowledgments

I would like to offer thanks to several people who have been instrumental in guiding and advising me through the writing of this book. First of all, I must thank my wife, Kristin, for her love, patience, and support throughout my career, of which this book is an important part. Very sincere thanks go to Dr. Stephen Kent and Dr. Harvey Krahn for their conscientious mentorship. They are the ones who first prompted me to ask the sorts of questions that made this manuscript a possibility. Thanks also to Dr. Reg Bibby for his collegial support and advice about navigating the publishing process. Thank you to the anonymous reviewers for their insightful feedback. Thanks to Glenn Wright and Amy Farranto, at Syracuse University Press, for their patience and their sound editorial advice. Last, but certainly not least, I would like to thank all the straightedge folks who shared with me their thoughts, perceptions, and experiences. Without your participation, this book simply would not have been possible. I wish you all the best.

# Straightedge Youth

# 1

## Introduction

### My Relationship to Straightedge

It is my primary goal in this book to illuminate the dynamics of an understudied youth (sub)culture known as straightedge. Straightedge is commonly described as a philosophy and a lifestyle characterized by abstinence from alcohol, drugs, casual sex, and even meat and animal products in some cases. While I do not actively identify myself as straightedge, it is a phenomenon that has impacted my personal and professional life in a number of ways since the 1980s, and it would therefore be misleading of me to pretend to be a completely neutral and detached observer. All researchers necessarily have at least some relationship with the people and issues that they study, and the nature of that relationship can pose limitations for the research process. I believe it is appropriate, therefore, for readers to begin with some understanding of my own relationship to straightedge so that they may have a better basis on which to consider and critically evaluate my claims and conclusions throughout this book.

Ironically, the very first time I heard the term *straightedge* was when I was eighteen years old and drunk at a house party. I was sitting on a couch next to a guy I hardly knew, and I asked him why he wasn't drinking. He explained that he was straightedge and that he didn't drink. His decision to abstain did not seem unusual or odd to me. Indeed, until I was seventeen years old, I never drank. When I was a child, my parents affiliated themselves for several years with the Church of Jesus Christ of Latter Day Saints, and Mormons are called to abstain from alcohol (among other things). Thus, as a child, alcohol certainly seemed like a bad thing from my point of view. As I grew into my early to midteens, I was consistently frustrated and saddened by my peers' apparent glorification of alcohol use. To me, drinking seemed weak, immoral, and dangerous.

In the summer before beginning grade twelve, on a camping trip, I took my first drink. Two drinks later I was, without a doubt, drunk for the very first time in my life—a cheap drunk indeed. Grade twelve proceeded to be a turbulent year in my life, as it is for many teens, no doubt. It was a year of questioning my identity, my life goals, my relationships, and above all my values and beliefs. It was a year of confusion. It was also a year of regular drinking with my friends, the beginning of a strong six-year addiction to cigarettes, and it marked my introduction to the hardcore/punk rock music scene in my home city. It was at the end of this year that I found myself drunk, at a party, and chatting on a couch with a straightedge abstainer.

The straightedge phenomenon became difficult to ignore as I immersed myself further in the local hardcore music scene during the early 1990s. Hardcore music was unlike any other music I had ever encountered. It was fast and intense. Similar to punk rock music, hardcore has a raw edge, characterized by driving, staccato, machine-gun drumbeats, fast, heavy guitar riffs, and simple repetitive bass lines. The vocalists typically shout or scream, and group chants and anthems frequently punctuate the lyrics. Borrowing from the heavy metal music genre, hardcore often breaks up the speed and intensity with interludes characterized by slower tempos, double bass drumbeats, and intricate guitar riffs.

The sound of hardcore was not the only attraction for me. The sonic qualities of the music, the lyrics, and the venues where I listened to the music all combined into one thematic package that seemed to articulate my life experiences. The music sounded angry and militant, and the lyrics always were moralistic, sociocritical, and preachy. I remember that the songs were about a number of different themes and topics, including social justice, hypocrisy, breaking with custom, and fighting back against the alleged corruption of society. Often the songs were also about straightedge. When I first heard Ian MacKaye (lead singer for the straightedge band Minor Threat) singing songs about the stupidity of drugs and alcohol, I could not help but be impressed. At the time, this music had something profoundly important to say to me. It was about personal power and social change. It seemed strong.

I began to pay closer attention to other straightedge themes in the music I was listening to: songs about "thinking straight"; songs about the weakness and moral degeneracy of teen culture; songs about the straightedge "family," or movement. I began to rethink my earlier teen perceptions of alcohol, and as I progressed into my early twenties I became acutely conscious of my own drinking and smoking. I gave up cigarettes and became a very casual and infrequent drinker. Even then, my drinking experiences were characterized by a low-key sense of guilt.

I remember in 1992 going to a gig featuring a local straightedge band called Blindside. At the beginning of the show, after the band had assembled its gear upon the stage, the lead singer addressed the audience: "Who here does drugs?" (A few calls and whistles from the audience.) "Yeah, well, fuck you! Drugs are for losers!" Directly following this condemnation, the band proceeded into its musical set. For almost an hour, the band played a series of short and speedy songs that addressed topics such as the alleged evils of drug use, unity among straightedge youth, social injustice, self-respect, and the necessity of fighting perceived enemies. As the musical set progressed, I noticed the slogans emblazoned on audience members' clothes. Compared to slogans I had observed at other punk rock or hardcore shows, many of these slogans were unusual and noteworthy: "Straightedge Youth: A New Direction," "Straightedge: Drinking Sucks," and "Straightedge: Watching You Fall Only Makes Me Stronger."

After this show, I began to explore straightedge further. I already listened to the music on a daily basis. I quit smoking and drank infrequently, and I even attempted vegetarianism. Nonetheless, I never (in my mind) officially became straightedge. It seemed to me a leap or a conversion that required a firm commitment. Straightedgers often described the transition to straightedge as akin to taking a vow or oath,

# Introduction

and I never felt that it was one that I fully could live up to or necessarily even wanted to live up to. In any case, as I entered my middle twenties and as other facets of my life occupied a more central position in defining my self-identity, straightedge progressively lost resonance with me, at least on a personal level. I continued to listen to hardcore music, but straightedge for me became mostly nostalgic.

As I finished my M.A. degree, however, I became increasingly interested in the idea of straightedge from an academic, sociological point of view. I began to wonder why some people become straightedge, and what was going on in their lives when they made that transition. I wondered too if the meaning of straightedge changed for them as time passed. Thus, in 1996 I began to search the academic databases for articles about straightedge, only to find that none existed. Apparently, at that time, researchers had overlooked the phenomenon. The few media accounts I found were cursory and stereotypical in their treatment of straightedge. Since then, a number of academic articles (two that I wrote) have appeared on the topic, with most of them appearing since 2003 (see Atkinson 2003; Haenfler 2004; Irwin 1999; Williams 2003; Williams and Copes 2005; Wilson and Atkinson 2005; Wood 1999a, 2003). These studies are to be commended for pioneering new academic insights into an interesting, diverse, and lamentably understudied subculture. Each study, however, either provides an overview of general straightedge norms, values, and beliefs (something the present study is trying to move beyond), or focuses on a relatively specific aspect of it. Thus, while it is encouraging to see a greater number of academic studies

5

appearing in the literature, there remains a need for an in-depth and comprehensive overview of the history and internal complexities of straightedge. For me, addressing this need constitutes the task at hand.

Having provided what is hopefully a convincing rationale for the present study, I wish to reiterate to readers, at the outset of this study, that I do not perceive myself as straightedge, and I do not consciously describe my lifestyle as straightedge. Neither, however, do I harbor any antagonism toward straightedge; my treatment of it certainly is not motivated by any kind of manifest political agenda (at least, none of which I am consciously aware). Indeed, straightedge is a phenomenon for which I retain some level of respect, and I have even problematized my own identity in relation to it. My general goal is to better understand straightedge and its adherents. I merely want readers to know that this goal did not emerge in a vacuum but is at least partially inspired by my own subjective experiences.

## What is Straightedge?

Historically linked to the punk subculture, straightedgers since the early 1980s have been distinguished by their committed and sometimes militant opposition to illicit drugs, alcohol, and perceived promiscuous/casual sexual activity (Atkinson 2003; Buckley 1996; Haenfler 2004; Irwin 1999; Krist 1996; Lagatutta 1996; Levinson 1997; Varner 1995; Williams 2003; Wood 1999a, 1999b, 2003). More recently, straightedgers are known for their highly political commitment to vegetarian or vegan lifestyles, as well as for their opposition to other perceived forms of animal exploitation (Haenfler 2004; Irwin 1999; Wood 1999a, 1999b, 2003).

The straightedge subculture is comprised predominantly of young men, along with a minority of women, in their late teens and early twenties, although some people claim a straightedge identity well into their thirties (Lagatutta 1996; Lahickey 1997). There are no rigorous estimates of membership currently available, but straightedge culture appears to be present in virtually all American and Canadian cities, as well as in numerous other major urban centers internationally (Irwin 1999; Lagatutta 1996; Lahickey 1997; Wood 1999a). Demographically, straightedge in North America seems to be largely, although not solely, a Caucasian, middle-class phenomenon (Lagatutta 1996), but issues of class and race tend to assume little manifest prominence in defining the boundaries of straightedge culture and identity, although, as I report later, some straightedgers do describe themselves as committed antiracists. Instead, diverging from the overt class and race bases of many other contemporary youth subcultures, straightedgers' sense of personal identity and group solidarity typically emerges from their perceptions of, and aversion to, abuses of drugs, alcohol, and sex among their peers and among the mainstream adult society (Irwin 1999; Lagatutta 1996; Wood 1999a, 2003).

Straightedge first appeared during the very early 1980s in the Washington, D.C., punk rock scene, where a number of punks were attracted to the ideas of Ian MacKaye, lead singer and songwriter for punk band Minor Threat (Wood 1999a). MacKaye's songs espouse disdain for the drinking, drug use, and promiscuous/casual sexuality that he perceived as common among other punks and among his mainstream teen peers during the late 1970s and early 1980s (MacKaye in Lahickey, 1997). Moreover, MacKaye's lyrics suggest that, by abstaining from intoxicants and casual sex, he possesses a mental and physical advantage, or a "straight edge," over people who indulge (Small and Stuart 1983). As Wood (1999a) points out, early straightedge music lyrics celebrate the ability to maintain control of oneself both mentally and physically. They also lament the perceived tragedy of young life wasted in destructive excesses of drugs, alcohol, and casual sex.

In addition to being a testament to his own personal perceptions and lifestyle choices, MacKaye's ideas apparently had the effect of mobilizing a latent sentiment shared by a critical mass in the American punk subculture. Supporting this claim, there is evidence that by 1982 self-proclaimed straightedgers and straightedge punk rock bands were appearing in punk scenes across the United States, espousing the lifestyle tenets of abstinence from intoxicants and casual sex (see Irwin 1999; Lahickey 1997; Wood 1999a). By the late 1980s, vegetarianism and veganism were emerging to assume a near-equal prominence as defining features of straightedge culture and identity (Irwin 1999; Wood 1999a).

Music and music scenes persist as a focal point for straightedge culture. Since the early 1980s, it has been common for members of the subculture to congregate and interact at punk rock music gigs featuring straightedge bands (see Irwin 1999; Lagatutta 1996; Lahickey 1997; Wood

# Introduction

1999a). Gigs enable straightedgers to visit with one another, to form new network ties, to hear straightedge music, to slam dance or mosh, and to purchase merchandise, such as compact discs, records, and T-shirts (see Irwin 1999). Since the early to mid-1980s, other influential music scenes in addition to that of Washington, D.C.—in Boston, Cleveland, Los Angeles, Memphis, New York City, Reno, and Syracuse—have spawned innovations in straightedge culture, as well as innovations in the sonic dimensions of straightedge music. As well as music gigs and commercially available music recordings, crucial "culture transmitters" (see Wood 2000) such as fanzines/magazines and straightedge Internet Web sites help to unite national and international straightedge culture (see Williams 2003; Williams and Copes 2005; Wilson and Atkinson 2005).

Straightedgers, both past and contemporary, symbolically demarcate their spaces, their media, and themselves with symbols resembling the letter X. Apparently, the X initially appeared during the very early 1980s, when it served as a mark used to distinguish adults from minors in punk-rock venues licensed to sell alcoholic beverages. It was customary for door staff in these venues to draw wide black Xs on the tops of minors' hands so that they could easily be distinguished by servers and bar staff (see Lahickey 1997; Wood 2003). Within a short period of time, however, straightedgers—who chose not to drink— had adopted the X as a symbol of both their identity and their solidarity with other straightedgers (see Lahickey 1997; Wood 2003).

The X persists today as a distinctive straightedge symbol. Even a casual perusal of straightedge media reveals that many followers sport artistic variations of the X on their clothes. Some even draw or tattoo the X on their bodies (Atkinson 2003; Wood 2003). Often, X symbols are flanked by slogans, such as "drug free," "true 'till death," or "only the strong," that communicate the wearer's subjective stance (Lahickey 1997; Wood 2003). Also, it is common to observe X symbols comprised of mainstream cultural objects superimposed. Some examples found on the covers of straightedge music recordings include crossed judge's gavels (see Judge 1989b), crossed baseball bats (see Diehard 1989), and crossed shovels (see Six Feet Deep 1994).

Despite the consistency of the X as a demarcating symbol of straightedge, styles of dress among straightedgers have endured much transition. Reflecting the subculture's roots, early straightedgers often sported a hardcore punk look consisting of shaved heads and military boots (Wood 1999b). Those in the late 1980s, however, often rejected hardcore punk styles, opting instead for hooded athletic sweatshirts and baseball caps (see Lahickey 1997). Contemporary straightedgers appear to blend largely with the pseudoalternative fashions of their nonstraightedge young-adult peers. Thus, while many contemporary subcultures, such as skinheads, impose rather strict and unchanging informal dress codes upon members, straightedge fashion seems to have been relatively fluid and diverse.

Even though straightedgers have been a part of American youth culture since the early 1980s, straightedge is a phenomenon of which most Americans remained completely unaware until the late 1990s. Moreover, the public's

# Introduction

introduction to straightedge culture took place under fairly sinister auspices. Public knowledge mainly came from mass media presentations of the extreme and brutal violence committed by a very small minority of straightedgers, mostly located in Salt Lake City, Utah, and Syracuse, New York (see Williams 2003). During the late 1990s, several television programs and newspapers reported stories about aggravated assaults and even murders allegedly committed by straightedgers against drinkers and drug users, stories that quickly marred the overall reputation of straightedge culture. Other than these sensationalized media accounts of brutal straightedge violence, together with a few small-scale academic studies, very little has been written about this subculture. Consequently, we are left with a rather skewed and one-dimensional picture of a phenomenon that is diverse and multidimensional.

## Research Goals

In light of the scant academic information on straightedge currently available and the biased media coverage of the phenomenon, I wish to conduct an empirically based and relatively comprehensive study of straightedge culture. This book presents an in-depth examination of aspects of straightedge culture that other academic studies have either overlooked or have touched on in only a cursory manner—specifically, the genesis of straightedge culture in the United States during the early 1980s, the major normative and ideological transitions occurring in straightedge culture since that time, and individuals' experiences and perceptions of what it means to be straightedge.

Gaining a comprehensive insight into such a multi-faceted and long-lived phenomenon is an ambitious task. Different individuals have correspondingly different under-standings of exactly what it means to be an authentic straightedger, and contemporary straightedgers may differ in crucial ways from those active in the straightedge scene in the mid-1980s or mid-1990s. Moreover, different cultural artifacts, such as music, symbols, and styles, may communi-cate divergent or partial meanings of straightedge. Thus, my examination of straightedge draws upon data collected from a variety of sources, each providing a slightly different window of insight. Specifially, I have taken a triangulated approach to data collection, using interviews with both past and contemporary straightedgers, content analysis of straightedge music lyrics, and semiotic analysis of its sym-bols. While it is not possible to exhaustively explore every single facet and nuance of straightedge culture, I hope at very least that this book can provide a reasonably compre-hensive and critical overview of the culture and the people who identify themselves in relation to it.

In exploring the specific dynamics of straightedge, the book also makes important theoretical contributions to our understanding of subculture. Much subculture theory im-plicitly paints subculture as a static phenomenon, implying that subcultures remain essentially unchanged over time and space. Other theories and studies, through a dispropor-tionate focus on common norms, values, and beliefs, inad-vertently homogenize subcultural identity and imply that all

# Introduction

members of the subculture form a roughly similar identity in more or less the same way. The findings presented in this book run directly counter to these common theoretical implications. Rather than being limited to such questions as "What is straightedge?" "What does it look like?" and "What constitutes a straightedge identity?" this book tends to ask instead, "How has straightedge changed over time and social space?" and "How does authentic straightedge identity differ among people who refer to themselves as straightedge?" In short, rather than focusing solely on the core values of straightedge or the common cultural referents that supposedly bind the subculture together, this book also explores the complexities and internal contradictions of straightedge. Indeed, complexity and contradiction are key themes needed to revitalize what has become a stagnant body of subculture theory.

# 2 Theory and Method

## Guiding Concepts

**S**everal perspectives and concepts guide and inform my examination of straightedge subculture, and it is important that readers be aware of these at the outset. These concepts will be referred to from time to time throughout the book. More importantly, they play an important part in informing my concluding theoretical discussion about complexity and change in subcultures.

### Frame of Reference

*Frame of reference* is a concept that readers will encounter frequently throughout this book. First coined by subcultural strain theorist Albert Cohen (1955), a subculture's frame of reference is a set of socially constructed definitions and "group standards" (Cohen 1955, 65). Stated simply, it is a set of overarching and guiding norms, values, and beliefs. For someone who begins to identify with a particular subculture, the frame of reference tells the prospective member what the subculture is all about as well as how to play the part of an authentic member of the group.

## Theory and Method

The subculture's frame of reference is a social or a cultural construct; it stems from the subjective experiences and social interactions of its members. In time, however, it may take on a seemingly objective existence independent of the human activity that created it in the first place. In other words, it "may achieve a life which outlasts that of the individuals who participated in its creation" (Cohen 1955, 65).

This tendency for a frame of reference to achieve autonomy from its creators is especially evident in contemporary subcultures, where norms, values, and beliefs become encoded into the subculture's texts, objects, symbols, styles, spaces, and rituals (see Fonarow 1997; Hebdige 1979; Weinstein 1991; Wood 1999a). Once encoded in these things, the subculture's frame of reference can be transmitted, long after its initial creators have left, to future prospective members. In turn, the frame of reference tends to shape or constrain future prospective members into a particular range of behavioral and attitudinal parameters. The prospective skinhead, for example, encounters a seemingly preexisting skinhead frame of reference, one that has been encoded in music, styles, and other cultural phenomena. While the subcultural identity is not entirely determined by the frame of reference, his or her identity is at least partially constrained by it.

Having made this assertion about the shaping power of the subculture's frame of reference, it is important to emphasize that the process is not unidirectional. Indeed, each new subculture member is impacted by the subculture's preexisting frame of reference, but each new member in turn acts back upon and changes it in at least a minute way. Thus, we can envision a subculture's frame of reference as something that perpetually evolves, so long as there are people who fashion their identities in relation to it.

This book explores the norms, values, and beliefs that define the general and changing parameters of straightedge culture. More importantly, it examines the ways in which individual straightedgers fashion and maintain an identity in relation to the subculture's shifting frame of reference.

*Mainstream Permeation and Exposure*

It is common for subculture theories and studies to focus on the ways in which subculture is different than or separate from mainstream culture. To be sure, most subcultures emerge at least partially in reaction to some aspect of the mainstream or dominant culture. Moreover, they often seek some level of insulation from the mainstream. Nonetheless, we should not overlook the ways in which the subcultures and mainstream culture are inextricably connected.

Arguably, David Matza was the first subculture theorist to explore connections between subcultures and mainstream culture. He was particularly critical of earlier strain perspectives for exaggerating the degree of separation between "deviant" and "conventional" cultural worlds (1964, 1969). According to Matza, subculture theorists tended to emphasize the ways in which subcultures were morally isolated or culturally autonomous from mainstream culture. This, he argued, induced a distorted understanding of subcultures.

## Theory and Method

According to Matza, a subculture cannot be entirely isolated or autonomous precisely because it exists within a wider mainstream cultural context that necessarily affects the subculture (1964, 37). Matza claims that its members invariably are encircled by the members of mainstream society in such contexts as school, neighborhood, work, church, and the mass media (46). Thus, although the subculture may provide at least partial insulation from the influences of the mainstream culture, the same subculture, as a result of its condition of encirclement, "necessarily reflects the permeation of conventional agents" (47). Subcultures, therefore, emerge and sustain themselves with a latent cultural support from conventional sources and traditions (63) and often reflect mainstream culture in important and significant ways.

Matza's ideas about permeation and exposure are important guiding concepts for parts of this book. Indeed, it is obvious that straightedge subculture does not exist in a social vacuum. On the contrary, all straightedgers to some extent are acculturated to mainstream society, and so their subculture may reflect and receive latent cultural support from mainstream society in important ways. It is not simply a coincidence that an antidrug youth subculture should emerge in the United States at a time when prominent politicians, celebrities, and other cultural agents were vehemently declaring a "war on drugs" in American society. As I explore further, much straightedge material culture of the 1980s, music lyrics in particular, reflected the mainstream "war on drugs" rhetoric in obvious and consistent ways.

# Straightedge Youth

*Symbolizing the Lived Experience of Contradiction*

The terms *cultural studies* and *Birmingham perspective* generally refer to the works of scholars from the Centre for Contemporary Cultural Studies at the University of Birmingham in England. Since the early 1970s, the notably broad contributions from the group have made a profound impact upon the study of subculture. Like the theories and perspectives that came before, Birmingham scholars recognize that subcultures emerge at least partially in reaction to mainstream cultural phenomena, and that furthermore they may reflect mainstream cultural phenomena in important ways. Compared with previous perspectives, however, the Birmingham perspective deeply politicizes the relationship. This distinctly political focus tends to emanate from the common theme among Birmingham studies that subculture emerges, fundamentally, from prospective members' lived experience of contradiction between the ideologies of mainstream society and the material realities of their social existence in that society.

In explaining the punk subculture, for example, these scholars observe that it emerged as something of parody and dramatization of England's ongoing economic austerity. Indeed, the 1970s English punk subculture emerged in an era where British working-class youth were tantalized by the consumerism of middle-class society, but where those same youth encountered recently unprecedented levels of unemployment, thus preventing them from attaining the lifestyles and the consumer goods that they were socialized to pursue. Reflecting this experience of contradiction between ideology and reality, British punk rock band The Buzzcocks described the state of affairs in 1976 as "all these livid things that you never get to touch" (The Buzzcocks, quoted in Savage n.d.).

In a dramatization of this conflicting state of affairs, British punks in the late 1970s allegedly championed all things that, from the perspective of respectable mainstream culture, were offensive, perverse, chaotic, and threatening (Brake 1993, 77–78; Hamm 1993, 29; Hebdige 1979, 106–7). Birmingham scholars note how this reaction to mainstream culture was symbolized through styles, music, and rituals. Punks, for example, would incorporate into their stylistic ensemble mainstream cultural artifacts that they had symbolically violated: shreds of school uniforms adorned with anarchy symbols, soiled and burnt pieces of the Union Jack flag; bizarre hairstyles that drastically deviated from the longish, neatly coiffured dominant style of the day; and standard household items, such as trash bags and safety pins, transformed into fashion accessories.

This book explores some of the external cultural phenomena and social contexts, such as the mainstream drug war, that shaped parts of the straightedge subculture and offered it latent cultural support. In addition, it needs to explore the ways in which straightedgers' lived experiences of those social contexts impact the way in which they form and maintain their identity. Moreover, it is important to consider the ways in which those lived experiences are symbolically encoded and displayed in the material culture of straightedge. Thus, further influenced by the theoretical contributions of the Birmingham perspective, parts of this book examine the ways in which straightedgers demonstrate their experiences, perceptions, values, and beliefs through such things as music, styles, language, and symbols.

## *Subculture as a Diachronic Entity*

According to Fine and Kleinman's often-overlooked interactionist theory of subculture, sociologists have tended to portray subculture as a homogeneous and static phenomenon, with self-evident boundaries, that one simply may enter into (1979, 2). In reality, however, subcultures are far from homogenous, their boundaries are often difficult to pinpoint with precision, and they are certainly not static in nature. On the contrary, according to Fine and Kleinman, subcultures are by definition internally heterogeneous due to the fact that they are composed of human beings, all of whom perceive and experience the social world in subjectively different ways.

They go on to state that "Each member's perspective on the shared knowledge of the subculture will necessarily be different from that of any other member. Therefore, even within a homogeneous group, action will require a negotiation of meaning, resulting in the continual production of socially constructed realities" (6). In other words, even though subcultures may be cemented to some degree by a commonly acknowledged frame of reference, each member's perspective and understanding of that frame of reference will necessarily be at least partially different. By extension, if each member understands it in a slightly different way, and if the subculture is created and sustained through the social interactions between its members, then the subculture and its frame of reference are, by definition, perpetually changing. Indeed, not only is the membership of the subculture in constant transition, but the frame of reference is continually being reconstructed and communicated to others.

This perspective holds crucial implications for the present study. It is especially important to realize that the straightedge frame of reference, and indeed the entire subculture, is a diachronic or perpetually changing entity. Not all straightedgers perceive, experience, and internalize the straightedge frame of reference in precisely the same way or to the same degree. Consequently, straightedge is an internally complex and sometimes internally contradictory phenomenon despite the existence of its frame of reference, which supposedly binds or cements the subculture into a cohesive cultural unit.

Thus, informed by Fine and Kleinman's interactionist perspective, this book investigates how being an authentic straightedger means different things to different people, and also how that meaning may change over time.

## Methodology

*A Case-Study Approach*

This book is best conceived of as a case-study analysis insofar as it strives for a comprehensive and historical representation of straightedge, and insofar as it incorporates a variety of divergent data sources to achieve that end. The power of the case study (and its importance for this project) lies in its ability to cope with social phenomena that are complex and prone to change. While many other research approaches facilitate the collection of cross-sectional, point-in-time data, the case study facilitates the collection of data that are multifaceted and historical in nature. Thus, a number of researchers and theorists concur that the case-study approach is the one best suited for exploring and revealing social processes (Mitchell 1983; Stoecker 1991; Yin 1984, 1992), and many scholars of subculture have employed a case-study approach. Bainbridge (1978), for example, reveals and elaborates processes of cultural implosion through his case-study analysis of the Process Church of Final Judgment. Similarly, Baron (1989) conducts a case study of the Canadian west coast punk subculture to explore processes of resistance to the dominant cultural ethos.

*Content Analysis of Straightedge Music Lyrics*

In those instances where a subculture survives well beyond the affiliation of its founding and early members, its researchers must surmount a methodological difficulty. While current members may harbor at least some awareness of the subculture's historical roots, they cannot testify directly to such moments or events. Consequently, the history of a subculture cannot adequately be gleaned only from interviews with its current members. Thus, when one seeks "snapshots" of a subculture at specific points of past time but cannot locate large numbers of early members, one must resort to examining the traces and clues that former members have left behind, notably the historical artifacts and texts that embody and communicate past subcultural themes. Arranged chronologically, historical subcultural texts may provide a series of frame-of-reference "snapshots." From such a series, the researcher may piece together at least a rudimentary history of the most general transitions undergone by the subculture over a given period.

Music lyrics comprise one of the more useful and readily available types of historical subcultural text. Irwin (1999, 369), in his own analysis of straightedge, suggests that "music may be seen as a barometer of changes in youth culture." Numerous other academics concur that subcultural music genres play an important role in affirming both conceptual and structural subcultural boundaries (see Baron 1989; Brake 1993; Dotter 1994; Hamm 1993; Hebdige 1979; Kinsella 1994; Laing 1997; Moore 1993, Ridgeway 1990; Walser 1997; and Weinstein 1991). In a study of the Canadian punk subculture, for example, Baron (1989) indicates that punk rock music communicates general punk subcultural themes. Weinstein (1991) similarly claims that subcultural music genres embody sets of codes or rules. Likewise, other researchers imply that music genres are important transmitters of subcultural attitudes and beliefs (see Brake 1993; Hamm 1993; Hebdige 1979; Kinsella 1994).

Using nonprobability purposive sampling techniques, I obtained the lyrics of more than six hundred songs recorded on seventy-three cassette tapes, compact discs, and vinyl records produced between the early 1980s and late 1990s. I verified recordings as straightedge (or straightedge-affiliated) upon the basis of their association with, or distribution by, self-professed straightedge record labels and distribution companies. In most cases, explicit references to straightedge within the lyric sheets or the presence of typical symbols on the album covers further verified the authenticity of selected recordings.

I analyze these primary sources according to Stake's (1994) model of issue development in case-study research. Initially, I perused straightedge music lyrics for general themes, and I based all subsequent data collection upon emergent thematic patterns and issues. I report thematic observations as assertions, and in the text of my study I support assertions with representative examples. Thus, through a process of thematic classification, I utilize straightedge music lyrics as means of identifying historical transitions in the broad ideals that seem to comprise the subculture's frame of reference.


*In-Depth Interviews with Straightedgers*

A substantial proportion of my data stems from in-depth interviews with twenty-one self-professed straightedgers and their affiliates. Like other subculture research using interview data (see Baron 1997, 1989; Widdicombe and Wooffitt 1990; Young and Craig 1997; Zellner 1995), this solicitation of insiders' viewpoints facilitates understanding of the meanings that individuals attribute to their actions and perceptions. Interview data buttresses my content analysis of music lyrics by yielding added insight into the normative and attitudinal boundaries of straightedge culture. More importantly, interview data allows me to investi-

## Theory and Method

gate how individuals create or maintain a straightedge identity, as well as how that identity might shift over time.

Because of the relative obscurity of straightedge, my
only practical recourse was to generate the interview sam-
ple using nonprobability snowball and purposive sampling
techniques. I began my sampling with a few informal
straightedge contacts and asked them if they would be will-
ing to pass on my contact information to other straightedgers. This technique of sampling, by means of informal
networks, generated nine respondents. I contacted the re-
mainder of the respondents via the Internet. There are several established and well-visited straightedge message
boards that I accessed over the Internet. I posted messages
on these boards, describing my research and requesting interested parties to contact me if they wished to learn more
about the research and possibly participate. This technique
generated an additional thirteen interviews. In total, I made
contact with about fifty straightedge individuals of whom
twenty-one agreed to interviews. Those not interviewed did
not take part for a variety of reasons, including being under
age, lacking access to a telephone, or simply not wishing to
participate. Some potential participants agreed to be interviewed but then failed repeatedly to make themselves
available.

I conducted all interviews over the telephone and
recorded the conversations using a modified tape recorder.
Interviews averaged approximately one hour in length and
were semistructured to the extent that I made a conscious
effort to explore a list of themes and probes that I had com-
piled into an interview schedule. Not all themes and

probes, however, proved to be relevant for each participant. Indeed, while there was a great deal of commonality among the experiences of my respondents, each person interviewed brought to the research a unique set of experiences and perceptions. Thus, although I utilized an interview schedule as a general guide, I made a concerted effort to be attuned to issues that the respondents identified as important and to follow up those issues accordingly. In order to render completed interviews amenable to analysis, all interviews were transcribed either by me or by a professional transcriber, who signed a confidentiality agreement.

Consistent with my goal of exploring subculture as process, I asked respondents about their transitions into a straightedge identity and their experiences with the subculture in general. I also asked respondents to describe the ways they maintain a straightedge identity, as well as about their interactions with others, both straightedgers and those outside the subculture. Thus, my interview data touches upon the ways in which respondents perform the role of straightedger in their everyday lives as well as the ways in which they manage their identity in the midst of other possibly competing identities.

Similar to my content analysis of straightedge music lyrics, I analyzed interview data according to Stake's (1994) model of issue development in case-study research. After conducting and transcribing the first ten interviews, I thoroughly read the transcriptions for the purpose of identifying emergent patterns and themes, which were used as a general guide for subsequent interviews. Throughout these interviews, however, I made a concerted effort to recognize and explore other novel themes and patterns as they emerged.

*Semiotic Analysis of Straightedge Symbols*

As explained earlier, straightedgers often demarcate themselves as well as their spaces with a distinct set of symbols based on the letter X. Moreover, the X apparently has endured a series of iterations and rearticulations intended to distinguish straightedgers in particular regions or to reflect and communicate a particular subjective stance. I have observed, for example, the X displayed as two crossed baseball bats, two crossed judge's gavels, two crossed straight razors (dripping with blood), and a wrench crossed with a hammer.

Semiotics refers to the study of signs and the way they work. According to John Fiske (1990, 40), semiotics comprises three main areas of study: (1) the sign itself (including the different varieties of the sign and the various ways it conveys meaning to the people who use it); (2) the codes or systems into which the signs are organized to meet the needs of the cultural group; and (3) the culture within which these signs operate. Using this definition as a general guide, I explore the X and its iterations coupled with a distinct focus on how individual straightedgers apprehend and utilize the X.

# 3  Music, Scenes, and Cultural Transitions

It is a well-established fact that music is a central aspect of many postwar and contemporary youth subcultures, be it the Teddy boys, mods, skinheads, or punks. Likewise, music plays an important role in shaping, communicating, and maintaining straightedge culture. Straightedge music obviously reflects the attitudes and beliefs of individual band members that play and produce it. Additionally, it reflects broader trends within the subculture, and it embodies a partial ideological framework that current and prospective straightedgers can refer to in maintaining their identity.

When one analyzes straightedge music chronologically, by the year it was produced, one quickly observes thematic trends that shift over time. For the purposes of the present chapter, I work from the assumption that thematic changes in straightedge music lyrics partly reflect broader transitions in the overall frame of reference and, by extension, changes in the boundaries and dynamics of the culture. This does not mean that straightedge music lyrics reflect the beliefs and behaviors of every individual straightedger. It simply means that they reflect some of the broader cultural trends emerging and disappearing among straightedge at different times and places throughout its history.

Thus, assuming that music lyrics can give some historical insight into what straightedge "looked like" in years and decades past, I intend this analysis as a type of lyrical history, tracing and illuminating some of the ways that straightedge has shifted over time.

## Does Music Really Matter?

While it is obvious that music can be a form of entertainment and personal expression, it is less clear whether it has a significant role in affirming or signifying straightedge cultural boundaries. Perhaps straightedge music lyrics merely are nothing more than personal expressions of the individual songwriters as opposed to being signifiers of broad cultural themes. Furthermore, it is plausible that a significant number of straightedge individuals simply do not care for the music at all. In light of these possibilities, and in anticipation of criticisms regarding validity, I think it is appropriate to address these issues.

I argue that music can be central to defining and maintaining straightedge cultural boundaries. Indeed, while a song embodies the subjectivity of the individual songwriter, that song is coercive upon other members of the subculture insofar as it evokes at least a small reaction, and in some cases a profound reaction, from the listener. In fact, of the straightedge individuals with whom I spoke, many reported that their introduction to straightedge was facilitated directly by music lyrics. For example, Neil explains: "I started listening to punk rock . . . and then I came across that Minor Threat album and that . . . whole straightedge song, and I was like, oh, that sounds kinda like me." Neil further states that, in many ways, he lived a straightedge lifestyle before actually encountering the idea of straightedge. He also claims that many of his friends did not make the same lifestyle choices as he did and that he felt a sense of loneliness as a result. His introduction to straightedge music provided him with a way of coping with and making sense of his feelings: "After I heard those songs, I was like, hey, someone else is the same as me."

Others reported similar experiences. Dan, a thirty-four-year-old who discovered straightedge in the early 1980s, explains: "The first time I heard the term *straightedge* was, of course, the Minor Threat song ["Out of Step]. A friend had loaned me a tape . . . so I am listening to this noise that I've never heard before. And what I could pick out was that 'I don't smoke, I don't drink, I am straightedge.' And I was like, wow, I don't do that either. There's a term for this!" Also commenting on the personal resonance and significance of straightedge music, Derek explains:

> I grew up on metal . . . and I'd, like, never heard of Earth Crisis and all those Victory [Records] bands . . . I mean they were really really good! . . . And I was blown away. I mean it was just this heavy brash music [with] songs about not doing drugs, and songs about veganism. . . . I really got into hardcore overnight. I was, like, wow, this is so cool! It's because like you listen to the lyrics, and

you go and buy a Minor Threat CD, you can relate to
everything being said.

Porcell relates a similar experience: "I heard about
straightedge bands like 7Seconds and Minor Threat, and I
was like, wow, this is something smart. This is something
positive, this is something progressive. So I latched onto
those early straightedge bands and it really hit home with
me." Thomas said that at the time he first identified himself
as straightedge, the music strongly resonated with his own
life experiences: "I just felt, like, very discontented and dis-
enchanted, and just didn't know where to turn or just what
the heck was going on. And that's what I always felt that the
music was all about. And I thought that the music actually
captured that feeling surprisingly well."

A straightedge woman named Vessel explained to me
that an affinity for the music genre, in some sense, is actually
a crucial defining characteristic of a straightedge identity: "I
think music, it's not only very important to me, but a big part
of straightedge because it did start in the music scene. . . .
part of straightedge is the music, and there's a difference between being drug free and being straightedge." Vessel goes
on to say that "within any culture there's different things that
the people within the culture have in common. And, with the
straightedge culture, one of the common grounds is music."

Thus, for at least some individuals, straightedge music is
crucial in facilitating the initial formation of a straightedge
identity as well as being important in the ongoing mainte-
nance of that identity. Not all self-professed straightedge
individuals are fans of the music genre, however. For exam-

ple, Sarah told me that "The only straightedge band I have is Minor Threat. . . . I'm not really into hardcore, it's a little bit too hard for me. . . . I've never been to a straightedge show, though I've been invited. It just didn't seem like something that I wanted to do." Another straightedge woman, Janine, says that she hears straightedge music only in passing: "I didn't care for the music that much. It wasn't really my kind of music, I guess." Twenty-nine-year-old Benjamin expresses a similar ambivalence:

> I think a big difference between me and other
> straightedge kids is that I'm really not a huge fan of
> straightedge music. . . . Most of the stuff I'm just not
> really into because I really don't like that metal stuff. . . .
> The chances are, if there's a straightedge show here I
> probably won't go. I might go, I might not go, whereas I
> think for a lot of other straightedge kids the music is like
> the central focus of the movement.

Thus, while music may be a crucial source of straightedge identity for many, there are some individuals who claim to maintain the identity without affiliating themselves strongly with its music genre or scene. For at least some individuals, therefore, themes predominant in the music genre may have relatively little impact on their identity.

## Emergence of a New Punk Scene

Observers consistently identify Washington, D.C., as the birthplace of straightedge, where Ian MacKaye, singer and songwriter for punk band Minor Threat, first articulated the straightedge concept in his lyrics. In "Another State of Mind," a documentary of the American punk scene released in 1983, MacKaye claims that straightedgers are a "new breed of punks" as he relates his teenage memories of other kids "getting stoned, throwing bottles, and driving fast." Referring to drinking and drug use, MacKaye adds that he "developed a deep hate for that lifestyle." When asked what it means to be straightedge, he replies, "I've got my head straight, my shit together, and I've got an advantage on you" (Ian MacKaye, quoted in Small and Stuart 1983).

In 1981, two Minor Threat songs (with lyrics written by MacKaye) served as particular catalysts for the emergence of straightedge in North America. In "Straight Edge," MacKaye sings about his perceptions of the stupidity of using drugs, as well as how drug use is a sign of personal weakness. He finishes the song with the following summarizing statement: "Never want to use a crutch/I've got the straight edge" (Minor Threat 1981a). MacKaye further elaborates these early sentiments in a song entitled "Out of Step": "I don't smoke, don't drink, don't fuck/At least I can fucking think" (1981b). In these lyrics, straightedge emerges as a lifestyle choice involving a rejection of common forms of alleged vice (i.e., drugs, alcohol, and casual sex). At a more general level, the above lyrical quotes communicate the importance of keeping one's mind and body free of impairing substances and practices.

Although for MacKaye the straightedge concept was an expression of his personal experiences and reflections, he explained that he very quickly realized that many other punks felt the same way he did:

## Straightedge Youth

The song, really, it resonated with a lot of people. A lot
more than I had ever imagined. I felt like people really
keyed in on that song, they really looked in on it.
Because I think there were a lot of punk rockers who
were straight, and who felt like, finally, here is someone
who's straight. . . . When the straightedge thing finally
came out, when the song came out, we started hearing
from people all around.

Not surprisingly, shortly after Minor Threat produced their
distinctly straightedge punk songs, other self-proclaimed
straightedge bands emerged in various parts of the United
States. As MacKaye explained:

I would say that we were the first band to sing about this
issue—punk band, that is. And then a band called SS
Decontrol from Boston. They kind of came on the
horizon and they were much more militant about it. And
then a band from Reno, Nevada, called 7Seconds. They
were much more kind of positive. . . . Those were the
first two. And then there were these other bands that
started to pop up from Los Angeles, like Uniform Choice
or America's Hardcore.

Without exception, these other early straightedge punk
bands echoed the themes that MacKaye sang about in 1981.
7Seconds (1984), for example, poses the following message
for the sexually promiscuous males among the hardcore
punk scene: "You fucking moron, your brains have run
amuck/A girl's only lot in life is not to fuck." Analysis of
other straightedge music lyrics indicates that opposition to

promiscuous sexual activity is a consistent point of concern throughout the history of the culture (see Billingsgate 1989; Earth Crisis 1995a; Judge 1988a; Youth of Today 1990).

Other straightedge songs more often emphasized the theme of thinking or being straight. In a song by DYS called "More Than Fashion," the lyrics state: "Straight mind, razor edge/Firm footing on a social ledge" (DYS, 1993a). Echoing this theme, Uniform Choice sings: "Straight and alert, straight and alert/Being high doesn't mean that much to me" (1985). Similarly, although at a later date, Youth of Today sings: "Life's full of conflicts, we'll face/We'll overcome them, thinking straight" (1986a).

These lyrical themes confirm that the earliest iterations of straightedge culture comprise a philosophy and corresponding lifestyle opposed to particular forms of alleged vice. Specifically, early straightedge music lyrics build upon ideas from Minor Threat lyrics and communicate the broad theme that drugs and alcohol (and casual sex, to a lesser extent) are a problematic aspect of youth culture insofar as they impose barriers to self-control and clear thinking. Music played a central role in transmitting these early straightedge ideals.

### Anti-Drug Militancy

As the straightedge scene began to grow in the later 1980s, the initial messages of "thinking straight" and "don't smoke, don't drink, don't fuck" began to take on new meanings and manifest themselves in slightly different ways.

One notable change, beginning in the mid—to late

1980s, involves the militant condemnation of drugs and drug users in straightedge music lyrics. Seemingly countless songs began to construe drugs as a dangerous social and moral threat (as opposed to a stupid personal choice) and often explicitly referred to drug users as enemies. Moreover, some lyrics prescribe violent confrontation as an appropriate response to the perceived problems engendered by drugs. In a song called "In My Way," Judge poses the following threat to drug users: "Those drugs are gonna kill you if I don't get to you first" (1988b). The band follows up this warning in a later song called "Bringin' It Down": "The needle, the track mark, you're scarred for life/You're weak, you're hurt, and you're gonna lose this fight" (1989a).

Other straightedge bands construct similar threats to drug users. Raid takes a particularly militant stance on the issue. In "Words of War," the band issues a warning to users of both legal and illegal substances: "Our war is on, the talk must quit/and all the guilty are gonna get hit" (Raid 1990a). The band similarly expounds a strong condemnation of tobacco smokers in a song called "Your Warning": "Death will be your outcome/Take This As Your Warning" (Raid 1991a).

These militant and seemingly violent lyrical condemnations of drugs and drug users are certainly not isolated cases among the straightedge music genre. In a song called "Bringin' It Back," for example, Integrity (1989a) reminisces about past confrontations with drug users: "BRINGING IT BACK, fists of truth/BRINGING IT BACK, wrapping that chain around their throats" (emphases retained from original lyric sheet). Echoing these themes several years later, in

a song called "Stra-hate Edge," One Life Crew (1995) similarly urges straightedge youth to rekindle the subculture's allegedly violent spirit: "Now it's time to put the HATE back in
straight edge/If you bring that shit around me, you're gonna
fucking pay" (emphasis retained from original lyric sheet).

Similar references among the genre are practically
countless, almost to the point of being cliché. Therefore, it
might be tempting for the casual observer to conclude that
the straightedge subculture is endemically violent and that
its individuals practice what is preached in the music. Such
a conclusion would be rash and likely incorrect. While
some straightedge individuals do practice violence, the vast
majority are nonviolent. Thus, in light of this probable contradiction between ideology (embodied in music) and action, and prior to discussing any further lyrical themes, it is
important to take a time out to critically discuss the practice
of using music lyrics as a data source.

## Music as a Problematic Statement of Real Behavior

There is certainly compelling evidence that elements of the
straightedge music genre, especially since the late 1980s,
have been rife with images of violence against drug users as
perceived enemies. On the basis of lyrical evidence alone,
however, it is naïve to assume that straightedge individuals
actually engage in the drug-war violence described in their
subculture's songs. Creating music is an expressive activity
and not necessarily an autobiographical testament. In fact,
there is evidence to suggest that at least some songwriters

intended their extreme lyrical depictions of violence merely as humorous exaggerations.

For instance, in something of a military chant that serves as a prelude to a song called "In Your Face," Slapshot (n.d.) satirizes straightedge themes of violence and moral condemnation: "Kill anyone with a beer in their hand, cause if you drink you're not a man/Straightedge, straightedge in your face, you don't belong in the human race." While this song allegedly evoked moral outrage from many listeners, the singer explained to me that he intended the song as a joke. In fact, according to Jack (whose stage name is Choke), the chant emerged partially from interscene competition between New York and Boston. Jack explained that he wrote the chant in a van while en route to a hardcore show in New York. He intended it to be humorous and to parody the toughness of both the Boston hardcore scene as well as the straightedge phenomenon in general. Nonetheless, humorous intentions aside, Jack explained how the purpose of the chant widely was misunderstood: " 'Kill anyone with a beer in their hand? If you drink, you're not a man'? I mean how ridiculous could you be? . . . Every interview was like, 'Do you really wanna kill people?' I said, 'Are you out your mind?' . . . It's sort of a problem with people in New York. They take themselves too seriously. I can't stand anyone who can't laugh at themselves."

Thus, violent music lyrics do not necessarily reflect actual violent behavior among the straightedge youth culture. A very small minority of straightedgers may engage in violent confrontations with nonstraightedge individuals. However, a vast majority does not endorse violence. Thus, reactionary music lyrics, such as those presented here, may be a form of expressive activity. Lyrics are thoughts, ideas, observations, and even artistic expressions that do not necessarily reflect real behavior.

## Vegetarianism and Animal Rights

As the 1980s came to a close, other new themes, previously unassociated with straightedge, began to emerge in straightedge music lyrics. One particularly noteworthy and lasting set of themes related to vegetarianism and animal rights. As a former member of Youth of Today, Porcell reflects about the appearance of the vegetarian theme among straightedge youth culture, as well as the power of music in effecting that theme:

> Me and Ray were both vegetarians, so we thought it was an important thing. Ray, he wanted to write a song about vegetarianism, and . . . it was such a foreign concept to most people, like, even within the hardcore music scene. We were even, like, oh God, do we really want to do this? Are people gonna take to this, or are they gonna take it, like, completely strange? And then, it was another idea whose time had come, because by the time we put out "We're Not in this Alone" [an album] and went on tour, so many people were vegetarian. And I think that it's a testament to the power of music. Music has such power to change and influence peoples' lives. It's amazing.

Porcell here refers to a song entitled "No More," which clearly espouses a provegetarian stance with the following lyrics: "Meateating, Flesheating, think about it/So callous to this crime we commit" (Youth of Today 1988a).

Following the example of Youth of Today, numerous other straightedge bands since the late 1980s also construe meat-eating as the moral equivalent of taking an innocent life: "A moral opposition, to the murder of animals/It's my philosophy, to take life is criminal" (Insted 1989). Similarly, on the topic of eating meat, Insight exclaims: "IT'S TIME to face the facts/THIS TIME END THE CRUELTY" (1990; emphases retained from original lyric sheet).

While a substantial proportion of music lyrics simply make a moral statement about animal rights, several bands advocated a directly confrontational stance against people who allegedly violate them. Indeed, some bands go so far as to claim that meat eaters should suffer the same consequence as the animals they eat. In a song called "Dead Wrong," for example, Integrity poses the following warning to meat eaters: "You've gone from being the hunter to being the hunted/You're dead" (1989b). Other bands also threaten a straightedge backlash against meat eaters. Worlds Collide (n.d.), for example, sings: "Your addicted action brings reaction/You'll suffer the fate of the flesh you fry." Similarly, according to a band called Burn (1990), meat eaters "have killed and shall be judged."

Lyrical condemnations of animal exploitation did not dissipate with the close of the 1980s. If anything, the 1990s brought lyrics even more condemning and reactionary, opposing animal exploitation in all of its perceived forms.

## Music, Scenes, and Cultural Transitions

Known as a particularly militant straightedge band, Raid offers the following warning to alleged animal exploiters in "Hands off the Animals": "All of their innocent suffering is real/Now it's time you learn just how the animals feel" (Raid 1990b). Raid further elaborates these threats in a song called "Under the Ax": "I'll remove you from birth and confine your every movement/Inject you with drugs as you drown in a liquid diet" (1991b).

Other straightedge lyrics of the early 1990s are nonetheless retributive in content. Syracuse-based band Earth Crisis has been championing the role of veganism in straightedge culture for the past fifteen years. In "Stand By," Earth Crisis constructs the following message for meat eaters: "You're a demon with blood on your hands/Your death will bring their freedom" (1992a). At a later date, Earth Crisis reemphasizes this message: "A bullet for every demon/Only your blood can cleanse you of your sin" (1995b).

In sum, lyrics indicate that, in addition to a perceived threat from drugs and drug users, the issue of animal rights became a fundamental element of the straightedge cultural ethos during the late 1980s and seems to have persisted. Having said this, I do not mean to claim that all or even most straightedge youth oppose drugs and alleged animal exploitation to the extent that selected lyrics might indicate. Indeed, many self-professed straightedge individuals are not vegetarian (or vegan), and most straightedge individuals do not advocate violence. However, even though lyrical themes do not necessary reflect the actions of all straightedge individuals, lyrics become part of a broader frame of reference that constrains or impacts, at least in a minute way, the identities of all people who consider themselves straightedge.

## Unity and Fragmentation

As a distinct straightedge scene began to take shape in the mid-1980s, music lyrics increasingly emphasized the theme of unity. Such a development certainly makes sense given the social context out of which straightedge was emerging. Straightedge emerged from a largely nihilistic punk scene that often championed the very lifestyle choices most straightedge individuals claim to abhor. As straightedgers became conscious of their identity at a more collective level, they sought to establish an identifiable set of boundaries for their scene and subculture.

DYS was among the earlier bands to emphasize the importance of straightedge unity, describing the subculture's youth as "a brotherhood, true 'til death" (DYS 1993b). In "City to City" (DYS, 1993c), the band depicts straightedgers as "united together, youth with a voice." The majority of other 1980s bands emphasized the unity theme in similar ways. Insted sings: "Bound together strong and true/Step by step is how it's done" (Insted 1988). Likewise, Youth of Today refers to the straightedge scene as one founded upon the united efforts and commitments of its youth: "Together we've built this, and all done our part/Together we've stood here right from the start" (1988b).

Twenty-eight-year-old Dawn, an active member of the New York and Connecticut straightedge scenes in the late

## Music, Scenes, and Cultural Transitions

1980s, confirmed the importance of unity when she explained to me how "hardcore kids" had a sense of being united in a sort of common ownership: "We're building something that's completely new and different and, you know, it's going to be a real alternative and a real way for people like us to exist in this world. We felt like we had ownership in this, you know what I mean? Like, you know, I helped, I am a part of this scene, and I *am* this scene in a way."

Despite straightedge emphases on the importance of unity, music lyrics and interview evidence suggest that the subculture began to experience some noteworthy internal tension during the late 1980s. More specifically, many early straightedgers apparently were beginning to transition out of the scene by starting to engage in the very lifestyles that they previously opposed. Reflecting such a trend, several long-term straightedgers cynically explained to me how many straightedge kids often are only "true 'till college" (as opposed to "true 'till death"). Porcell clearly touched on this theme when he discussed his disillusionment with the straightedge scene in the early 1990s: "I was playing with Gorilla Biscuits at the time, who were like a big straightedge band. . . . They were straightedge early on, but they were getting older. None of them were straightedge [anymore]. We'd go on tour and sing these straightedge songs, and none of the kids that used to have Xs on their hands . . . were straightedge anymore."

Reminiscent of Porcell's discontent, lyrical condemnations of defectors became common in straightedge music of the late 1980s and early 1990s. Much of this disapproval reflected feelings of disillusionment and frustration about youth who were perceived to have abandoned the philosophy and lifestyle. Bold (1988a) sings: "You talk big, when you preach/But empty promises are what you keep." Echoing this reference, and even referring to straightedge apostates as "backstabbers," Youth of Today says: "Stabbed us all in the back/Right in the back!/Don't you dare look me in the eye!" (1986c). Similarly, Judge sings: "We have seen the backstab blood/Most came and fuckin' went" (Judge 1988c). Earth Crisis further exemplified the subculture's disenchantment with straightedge apostates: "Fuck all those who bent the straight edge with their fucking lies" (1992b). Other bands went so far as to threaten "backstabbing" straightedge youth with a violent retaliation. Confront directs the following threat to alleged backstabbers in a song entitled "Payday": "You're the one that's gonna pay/Getting beat is the only way"(1993).

In sum, lyrical and eyewitness evidence confirms that straightedgers in the mid—and late 1980s were seeking to establish and preserve a sense of unity and belonging among the members of their subculture. Around the same period, however, evidence also suggests that the subculture experienced internal tension caused by the perceived defection of some individuals. Whether tension and defection equally characterized all regional scenes and franchises is difficult to ascertain. Indeed, some observers purport that certain scenes were more fragmented than others. Jack, the lead singer for Slapshot (a Boston-based band), commented to me about the New York hardcore scene in particular, claiming: "They always had a disjointed, backstabbing scene. . . . and it's still that way today." Further into our conversation, Jack suggested that some of the interscene tension may have been generated by the efforts of certain bands and individuals to color the definition of straightedge in ways that reflected their own subjective perceptions: "I always thought straightedge should be for everybody. It should be as easy as it possibly can be. A lot of guys decided that they wanted to make it their own little club."

## Hardline Resurgence

Reflecting Jack's discontent about people seeking to make straightedge more stringent and exclusive, a new variation on the subculture began to emerge during the late 1980s and early 1990s, one that distanced itself from mainstream straightedge. This new variation is commonly known as *hardline straightedge,* or simply, *hardline.* Initial lyrical references to hardline typically referred to the level of militancy of one's "claim" or identity as straightedge. Confirming the relationship between hardline and militancy, Porcell comments on his perceptions of early permutations of hardline mentality:

> One of the next trends was sort of this hardline, tough-guy, I-am-gonna-kick-your-ass-if-you're-not-straightedge type thing. . . . I can really see where the mentality comes from. Especially growing up in the skinhead scene in New York City, people throwing beer cans at you. In high school, people making fun of you for being straightedge. I can see it as a reactionary thing. I even

did this record, Project X, and it was a real hardline straightedge record. Like, we had this one song and the lyrics were: "I am as straight as the line that you sniff up your nose/I am as hard as the booze that you swill down your throat/I am as bad as the shit you breathe into your lungs/and I'll fuck you up as fast as a pill on your tongue." And I mean, whatever, at the time, that's the way I felt. But then, as we went on and we would like play and stuff, I saw what a negative reaction this had on kids. . . . And it was like, this has to stop. I felt bad because I felt like I was actually promoting it with records.

By the early 1990s, hardline was a fairly widespread and well-known presence in the straightedge music scene. Suggesting that hardline had emerged in reaction to weakness and lack of commitment among mainstream straightedgers, Raid sings, "Don't limit your potential through an X/Develop a superior conscience." Furthermore, stating their hardline identity, and placing themselves in opposition to nonhardline straightedgers, Raid sings: "Forget the past, it's time for the new school, the hardline/So now you're going to see why you're our enemy" (1990c). Finally, Raid seemingly epitomizes the hardline sentiment in a song called "Unleashed": "Straight in your face, my law pure and strong/Live tough on a pledge, in a world full of wrong" (1990d).

Other texts, apart from music lyrics, occasionally outline hardline in a more formal and movement-oriented way. A manifesto, distributed by a group claiming to be

## Music, Scenes, and Cultural Transitions

Bloomington Hardline, offers the following goals, ideals, and definitions:

> The ultimate goal of hardline, however unrealistic, is to revolt against the present system and tear it apart in the name of supreme justice. . . . a victory for hardline is a victory for nature, for we intend to take the earth back to a system of living with nature and not against it. For too long the greedy hands of evil have forced us to live by their rules, and we will no longer stand for your defiance of the basic laws of the earth. No more eating of our animal brothers and sisters. No more scientific death camps for the unborn victims of selfish sexuality. No more abusing the body with drugs that weaken our minds and make us tools No more excuses, the earth must be set free. . . . To stand for justice is to stand for all that is hardline, and to stand for hardline is to stand for justice. . . . Hardline cannot compromise itself to those who do not believe in all parts of its ideology. You believe in it all or none.

Here, hardline appears to be a sort of orthodox reconstruction of straightedge culture. In addition to the historical focus on drugs, this manifesto places hardline squarely amidst more recent issues such as animal rights, abortion, and environmental awareness.

Since the early 1990s, mainstream media have been quick to characterize hardline as representative of straightedge culture in its entirety. Rumors abound about the proliferation of hardline violence. In reality, however, hardline comprises only a minority of the straightedge subculture (despite the existence of hardline lyrics, manifestos, photographs, and media coverage). Ian MacKaye relayed to me several of his observations that partially confirm the minority status of hardline as well as the media's misrepresentation of its magnitude: "What aggravates me so much about all of this is that I think, within straightedge, for every kid that blows up a fur factory, there's like ten thousand kids who are just trying to do the right thing in their own lives. And they're just not newsworthy."

## The Importance of Straightedge Music Scenes

The overall shape of the straightedge subculture is often influenced by themes that emerge initially in small and localized music scenes. Influential local music scenes represent a sort of critical mass. Both the followers and the bands active within those scenes sometimes create and disseminate profound ideas through their music that influence and even steer the development of the entire subculture. Throughout the straightedge subculture's twenty-five-year history, there have been several such influential music scenes, and it is important that they receive at least some level of discussion in this book.

Undoubtedly, the most influential of all straightedge music scenes is the one that took place in Washington, D.C., in the early 1980s, led by local band Minor Threat. The ideas of singer Ian MacKaye apparently had the effect of mobilizing a latent sentiment shared by a critical mass locally and later throughout the United States during the early 1980s. Commenting on the fact that his ideas became a powerful mobilizing force, MacKaye explained that he is actually very surprised that the straightedge concept developed beyond his song "Straight Edge": "I think that it's really important to note that I was singing to fifty people, or maybe one hundred, or maybe even two hundred. But I wasn't thinking that it [straightedge] would be something that people all around the country or the world would pick up, or that it would be an idea that would be discussed for more than [twenty years]. It's crazy."

As MacKaye's initial message spread, it seemingly resonated with people in other American punk scenes, the members of which often rearticulated the straightedge concept in a number of influential ways. Readers may recall that members of the Boston, Reno, and Los Angeles scenes allegedly injected certain subjective spins or interpretations of the early straightedge ideal into their music. One particularly influential scene of the mid—to late 1980s was thriving in New York City. Indeed, many early observers credit the New York scene with providing the momentum that transformed straightedge from a punk minority to formal subculture in its own right.

According to MacKaye, straightedge bands from the New York area were crucial forces behind the consolidation of a distinct straightedge scene and culture:

It wasn't until the New York scene in about 1984 or 1985 [that] there was an explosion [in the straightedge music scene]. And again led pretty much by Youth of Today, what was referred to as New York straightedge hardcore. And that's really where the modern notion of

the movement was born. Ray Cappo, who was the
singer of Youth of Today, I guess he was really a
charismatic person. . . . He was really the one who
articulated straightedge in a militant, formalized,
movement way.

Members of Youth of Today make similar claims about
their influential status. Porcell (guitar player and cofounder)
explained how the band consciously sought to become a
rallying point for straightedge: "Being influenced by bands
like Minor Threat, and Youth Brigade, and 7Seconds, and
these bands that really had a lot to say and lot of criticisms of
the way that American life is set up. Just being influenced by
that, we wanted to be in a straightedge band. We wanted to
be in a band with a positive message that could actually impact kids, like these other bands had impacted us."

In disseminating this "positive message," Youth of
Today, like all straightedge bands of the day, communicated
the importance of abiding by the subculture's traditional
lifestyle tenets. However, along with other New York bands,
Youth of Today helped galvanize the subculture into a more
formally identifiable entity by communicating themes of
pride, commitment, unity with other straightedgers, and op-
timism about the power of youth. Indeed, their self-
referencing song entitled "Youth of Today" neatly sums up
what the band was all about: "Physically strong, morally
straight—Positive youth, we're the youth of today" (1986b).

Since the late 1980s, other straightedge music scenes
have also powerfully influenced the direction and development of the culture. The scene in Syracuse, New York, is one

that has been especially influential, not to mention notorious. Commonly known for its particularly militant brand of straightedge, Syracuse is known also as the birthplace of the immensely popular straightedge band Earth Crisis. Formed in the early 1990s and fronted by lead singer Karl Buechner, Earth Crisis is often acknowledged as a musical vanguard of hardline straightedge. The band was not in fact the first vegan straightedge band; in the late 1980s, Raid and Vegan Reich, two bands based in Memphis, Tennessee, allegedly became among the first to champion veganism. However, Earth Crisis is regarded as a major inspiration for what is sometimes called the "vegan straightedge movement" (see Earth Crisis 1992c).

As I discussed earlier, Earth Crisis's music lyrics are notorious for their frequent depiction of brutal violence committed against drug users, meat eaters, and straightedge backstabbers. However, such depictions are likely nothing more than creative expressions as opposed to depictions of actual behaviors and events involving straightedgers. Nonetheless, despite the low likelihood that Syracuse straightedgers actually engage in the violence depicted by the local bands, casual observers and the media alike have time and again stereotyped them as a particularly militant and violent element of the broader subculture.

One observer posted the following statement about Syracuse straightedgers on an Internet Web page: "Hardcore scenes like the one in Syracuse, New York, have led to some serious incidents of violence, since the beer-loving Syracuse jocks conflict with the beer-hating Syracuse straightedge jocks. So I say fuck these neo-straightedge "hate-edge" Nazi knuckleheads, who go around preaching and hurting people. They really may as well be Nazis" (Anonymous n.d.).

Other observers, however, paint a very different picture of the Syracuse straightedge scene. In an online interview, Justin Guavin, long-time member of the scene and cover artist for Earth Crisis album covers, had this to say:

> The funny thing is, people have always said that "Syracuse kids hate anyone who isn't straightedge or vegan, and want them beaten or killed." This is the most absurd thing I have ever heard, and has *never* been the case. We have all always had tons of friends that were neither straightedge nor vegan. I mean, it's just a complete fantasy. Nobody ever got beat up at Syracuse shows. We never beat anyone up for smoking or drinking. . . . I would always hear about kids scared to come to Syracuse for shows because they had heard all these horror stories, like shotguns at shows and shit, and I would just crack up. But, it was really disheartening at times to have all this said about you that just isn't true. I mean, we built an incredible scene, Syracuse was many bands' favorite place to play, straightedge or not. And, it just kind of sucked to have this rep that was not deserved. . . . I mean, in New York City or New Jersey at the time, sometimes you could get beat up just for . . . not being from there. We never had anything like that going on. (How's Your Edge n.d.)

Other observers affirm Guavin's perception of the scene as largely nonviolent. In a 1996 *48 Hours* documentary, a number of Syracuse-area straightedgers are asked about the meaning of straightedge. Rather than emphasizing violence, they very clearly explained that the subculture is, above all, about respect: respecting one's body, and respecting others (Lagatutta 1996).

While many will refute depictions of violence as a characteristic feature of the Syracuse scene, stereotypical depictions of violence have nonetheless real consequences for some of the scene's followers. Some, like Justin Guavin, point out the negative and demoralizing effect that violent stereotypes have upon him personally and upon the Syracuse scene more generally. Others, like Karl Buechner, experience much greater and disruptive sorts of consequences. For example, in an interview with an online straightedge fanzine, Buechner explains that the negative images associated with the Syracuse straightedge scene garner such suspicion from outsiders that he and others have actually been confronted and "harassed" by ATF agents in addition to other agents of social control (*Value of Strength* #4 n.d.). Undoubtedly, such official attention serves to reinforce existing public opinions and perceptions of Syracuse straightedgers as a violence-prone element of the broader subculture. Moreover, such attention directed towards particular music scenes likely facilitates a skewed or biased public image of the entire subculture, both nationally and internationally.

In sum, local music scenes are a crucial generating force for new subcultural innovations, and local music scenes furthermore can play a key role in shaping the public image of the straightedge subculture in its entirety. Scene-based innovations ensure that the broader norms, values, and beliefs (which generally define the parameters of the subculture) will be perpetually in a state of flux, transition, and development. Unfortunately, however, the more prominent, vocal, or reactionary scenes may also be the ones most easily observable and identifiable to the nonstraightedge public. Consequently, as such straightedge music scenes garner a disproportionate level of attention from the public, the media, and mainstream agents of social control, they may inadvertently misrepresent the characteristics of the broader straightedge subculture.

## Krishna-core

As some youth were looking to hardline as a beacon of straightedge culture, others in the late 1980s and early 1990s were looking to radically different belief systems to revitalize their straightedge commitment. More specifically, beginning in the late 1980s and gaining rapid momentum during the early 1990s, straightedge youth in increasing numbers began to align themselves with the teachings of the Krishna Consciousness movement (Wood 1999a).

At first glance, one might think it strange to observe a connection between these two cultural phenomena. However, if one examines the central lifestyle tenets that all devotees of Krishna are obligated to follow, one will very quickly see striking similarities. Specifically, Krishna devotees are called to abide by the following lifestyle tenets: (1) No eating of meat; (2) No illicit sexual activity; (3) No consumption of intoxicants; and (4) No gambling. Thus, at least on the surface, Krishna Consciousness is a religious belief system that is compatible with a straightedge lifestyle.

The popularity of Krishna ideology and its compatibility with straightedge is evident in the abundance of Krishna Conscious hardcore, or Krishna-core bands, which seemed to explode onto the straightedge music scene in the early 1990s. Notable examples include 108, Another Wall, Copper, Prema, and Shelter.

Like straightedge music, Krishna-core encourages opposition to drugs, animal exploitation, and promiscuous sex (see Shelter 1997, 1993). Diverging thematically, however, Krishna-core places a heavy emphasis on the allegedly "illusory" nature of material existence. In a song called "Destiny," for example, Prema sings: "We accept illusion, along with false identity/But only to complicate our path to true destiny." Also communicating a belief that material existence merely is an illusion, 108 sings: "I know your world is nothing/I turn my back on your corpse hearted 'reality' "(n.d.). In a similar vein, Shelter says the following about material human existence: "This world's like a dream, it's not what it seems/You think its solid but it fades instead" (1992a).

Apart from music lyrics, other subcultural texts disseminate the theme that material reality is illusory. Shelter's (1992b) *Quest for Certainty* compact disc includes a printed sermon that states: "The actual form of life for living entities is one of spiritual happiness, which is real happiness. This happiness can be achieved only when one stops all materialistic activities. Material sense enjoyment is simply imagination."

## Straightedge Youth

While to a certain degree straightedge is also about rejecting material-sense pleasures, Krishna-core literature often describes straightedge as a lifestyle and movement that will ultimately fail to satisfy. An article in *War on Illusion*, a Krishna-core magazine, explains the futility of the straightedge philosophy and lifestyle when it is practiced in a nonspiritual way:

> Straightedgers realize that sense gratification won't satisfy them. The problem is they don't know what *will* satisfy them. . . . Since the living entity is by nature spirit, when he engages in spiritual activity, or Krishna Consciousness, he finds the true bliss, peace, and contentment that he's constantly searching for. And if he's found true happiness and satisfaction, what need does he have to dig back into the mire of false pleasures? (Porcell n.d., 17)

Thus, for a large segment of the straightedge subculture, Krishna Consciousness appeared as an answer suggesting that straightedge goals could be best realized when pursued in a more spiritual way. For some individuals, Krishna Consciousness simply made sense. It allowed straightedgers essentially to remain straightedge, but it also sanctified their lifestyle choices, suggesting that they were already well on the path towards enlightenment. Viewed in this context, it is certainly not difficult to understand how at least some straightedgers found Krishna Consciousness highly appealing.

In addition to the close links between respective

lifestyle tenets, the straightedge subculture and Krishna Consciousness appear to be highly compatible in at least one other respect. In particular, close scrutiny of the straightedge music genre reveals connections between each group's philosophy on human existence. The Krishna Consciousness movement embraces the Hindu belief that human existence progresses historically through distinct ages called Yugas. According to this theory, humankind now lives in the Age of Kali, or the Kali-Yuga, which supposedly is the period directly prior to the termination of humankind's material and allegedly illusory existence (Judah 1974, 129). Purportedly ruled by the goddess Kali (a powerful, fierce, and terrible goddess capable of immense and indiscriminate destruction), sources describe the Kali Yuga as an evil age characterized by sickness, degeneracy, and indulgence in sense pleasure (Judah 1974, 129; Prem Nath 1995, 239). The Kali Yuga concept may be highly appealing to some straightedge youth, who perceive a world plagued with addiction, sense pleasure, and the "murder" of animals for human consumption.

Indeed, music lyrics and other cultural artifacts indicate that some straightedge youth, who seemingly do not identify themselves as Krishna Conscious, nonetheless explicitly identify with the Kali Yuga concept. For example, conforming to typical descriptions of Kali as a black-skinned goddess with a tusked and blood smeared face, a third eye, and wearing a necklace of human skulls (Prem Nath 1995, 239), Integrity prints a picture of the goddess upon the front cover of an album, *In Contrast of Sin* (Integrity 1989d). Furthermore, their song by the same title refers to life in contemporary society as "this age of Kali" (1989c). Similarly, Mean Season (1994), in a song entitled "Four Circles: Kali," describes life in contemporary Western society as a degenerate "plague of humanity."

In sum, while it would have been difficult to predict when straightedge first appeared in the early 1980s, Krishna Conciousness nonetheless emerged as a recognizable and seemingly significant force among the subculture in the early 1990s. For many straightedgers, it appeared as a highly straightedge-compatible religious belief system, and the boundaries of straightedge culture permutated once again as a result. Krishna Consciousness, however, was not the only spiritual belief system to have an impact on straightedge. As some sought Krishna, others sought inspiration in ideas and teachings aligned with Satanism.

### Satanic Themes and Imagery

Beginning in the early 1990s, and gaining momentum initially among bands in the Cleveland hardcore scene, elements of the straightedge music genre began to communicate themes and images that many would describe as Satanic in nature. Early references were moderately obscure and consisted mainly of Christian images of the apocalypse, albeit one where God has abandoned humankind. For example, in a song rife with religious imagery of hell, denial of redemption, and the general destruction of humankind, Integrity sings: "Somewhere out there watching/Your savior starts to laugh" (1991a). During another song, Integrity again constructs images of God abandoning humankind: "Brought up from the depths of hell/The changing lamb turns to sand" (1991b). Invoking similar imagery, a band called Ringworm, most of whose members previously belonged to other straightedge bands, sing: "I have touched the face of God, and it is cold, it is dead" (1993a). In another song, asserting that humankind presently lives in "the witch's season," Ringworm implies the need for mass human extermination: "The cleansing of humanity is the chore, the instrument is the irony of holy war" (1993b).

References and images suggesting a need to "purge" humankind appear frequently in other straightedge texts also. Integrity prints a startling image upon the band's *Humanity Is the Devil* album cover (1996). Under the caption "Holy Terrorism," there is a cherubim likeness of Charles Manson, his forehead marked with an X (not a swastika), riding upon a saddled fish. Printed on the cover are the following words: "You enter this world in pain, and shall leave in the same vein."

Into the middle 1990s, elements of the straightedge music genre began to explicitly refer to the teachings and images of an obscure and arguably Satanic religious group called the Process Church of Final Judgment (see Bainbridge 1991, 301–4). According to the Process Church, humankind has doomed itself through its inherent and unchecked corruption and now lives amidst the apocalypse prophesied in the Book of Revelations (1997, 250–51). Moreover, the group communicates a belief that the events of the apocalypse stem from a pact between the alleged gods Jehovah, Lucifer, Christ, and Satan (Bainbridge 1997, 245; 1978, 170).

## Straightedge Youth

Reflecting this apocalyptic belief, Process religious meetings typically involved the following announcement: "Through Love, Christ and Satan have destroyed their enmity and come together for the End, Christ to Judge, Satan to execute the judgment . . . Christ and Satan joined, the Lamb and the Goat, pure Love descended from the pinnacle of Heaven, united with pure Hatred risen from the depths of Hell. . . . The End is now. The New Beginning is come" (Bainbridge 1997, 245).

Other Processean publications depict a more sinister image of a supernaturally conspired apocalypse. According to an electronic pamphlet entitled "Satan on War,"

The final march of doom has begun. The earth is prepared for the ultimate devastation. The mighty engines of WAR are all aligned and brought together for the End. The scene is set. The Lord LUCIFER has sown the seeds of WAR, and now weeps to see them take root and flourish in the fertile ground of man's destructive nature. The Lord JEHOVAH decrees the End and the violence of the End. He prophesies the harvest of monumental slaughter. And I, the Lord SATAN with My army of the damned, am come to reap that harvest, and to feed My furnace with the souls of the fearful. (The Process n.d.)

During 1996 and 1997, a straightedge record and distribution company disseminated pamphlets that directly echoed such Processean beliefs about humanity's inherent corruption and the imminence of a divinely conspired apocalypse. Written by the self-proclaimed Holy Terror Church of Final Judgment, these publications claim that Jehovah and Satan have conspired together in a plan to destroy humankind. Moreover, claiming that the world soon will come to an end, Holy Terror publications state that all humans should participate in the world's demise. Packaged with an Integrity CD (see Integrity 1996), a Holy Terror pamphlet entitled "Humanity Is the Devil" explains: "Humanity chose to disregard Jehovah's generous wager. Your humanity chose sense pleasure over eternal salvation. Now you must live with your choices." Further reflecting Processean teachings, the pamphlet describes, in detail, that "the lamb and the goat have finally fused as one." More specifically, it explains that Jehovah and Satan, at the request of Jesus Christ, have engaged in a mutual pact to destroy humankind. The unknown author says also that demons in human form already are living among humankind, preparing for its destruction. Thus, the pamphlet urges readers to "identify the demon, and then destroy them before they destroy you."

Further articulating Process ideas about the individual's role in the world's demise, a 1997 *Victory Megazine* article entitled "Release the Fiend" states:

> Know that life is worthless unless it is lived in the very teeth of death, that peace is nothing more than a fleeting moment in the midst of war, that love is empty save as a transitory oasis in a world of violent hatred, that to create is only meaningful in order to destroy. . . .
> Choose what road of slaughter you will follow. Then stride out upon the land amongst the people. Kill with

the devastating precision of your sword arm[,] . . .
destroy with the overwhelming fury of your bestial
strength, lay waste with [the] all encompassing majesty
of your power. (Abernathy 1997)

All of these straightedge publications are adorned with
Process symbols and imagery. Allegedly symbolizing power
(Bainbridge, 1978, 186), the typical Process symbol consists
of four interlocking bars, which resemble concurrently both
a swastika and the letter *P.* Integrity displays variations of
this symbol on three different album covers (see Integrity
1996, 1997a, 1997b) in the form of a lamb and goat fused
together at the legs. This fusion supposedly symbolizes a
pact between the forces of good and evil.

These allusions to evil and the mass destruction of humankind may embody an extreme consolidation of the
straightedge subculture's opposition to the perceived social
and moral degeneration of Western society. However, these
themes should not necessarily be taken as conclusive evidence of some sort of straightedge faction. Indeed, upon
closer examination, it appears that they stem predominantly
from bands in the Cleveland, Ohio, area, and from Integrity
in particular.

Dwid, the lead singer from Integrity, explains that he
simply finds the Process Church an interesting phenomenon: "There are so many speculations regarding the
Process. There are several alleged connections between the
Process and certain serial killers. . . . There are many sides
to the Process, but the destructive side of it is what interests
me. . . . I'm definitely attracted to Satanism. I am interested

in the destructive and animalistic side of who I am. I think mankind is an abomination. . . . For lack of a better word, Satanism is the most appropriate term I can think of to describe how I feel. I am more of a predator than a pacifist" (Dwid, cited in *Terrorizer Magazine* 1997). In a 1997 interview with *Metal Maniacs Magazine,* Dwid further suggested that his lyrics are highly personal in nature and that he is "not calling for people to commit crime sprees" (Dwid, quoted in *Metal Maniacs Magazine* 1997).

While songwriters may claim that their use of satanic imagery is highly personal in nature, evidence suggests that at least a few isolated straightedge individuals are "dabblers in Satanism" (see Zellner 1995). A 1994 issue of the straightedge fanzine *Inside Front,* for example, includes an interview with a former straightedger who claims now to be a Satanist. The interviewee explains that he distanced himself from the straightedge subculture because he perceives that its philosophies and lifestyles are "obsessive" in nature. Moreover, he professes his adherence to the alleged satanic tenets of "do unto others as they do unto you, be aware of your surroundings, and value yourself." During a separate interview in the same magazine, an anonymous member of Lash Out, a straightedge band, refers to Satanism as "a positive ideology" (quoted in *Inside Front* 1994).

At least one straightedge individual with whom I spoke expressed an interest in Satanic themes. During an interview, he explained that he does not abide by any particular religious codes, but that he emphasizes themes such as "self empowerment, think for yourself, do your own thing." He further explained that he glanced through Anton Lavey's *The*

*Satanic Bible* and concluded that the book is really about "doing your own thing." This individual, however, in no way labels himself as a Satanist. Instead, he explains that his stance on life involves "[not] hurting people in a direct sense, and don't worry about what other people are gonna say."

In sum, while there is very likely not a full-blown or organized Satanic straightedge faction, Satanism is an ideology that appears to resonate with at least some current and former straightedge people on at least a superficial level. Insofar as Satanist and Process teachings emphasize themes of personal power, self-preservation, and/or hatred of one's enemies (see Bainbridge 1997, 1978; Lavey 1969), straightedge youths' attraction to these teachings at least partially become clear. Such ideals provide them with a conceptual vehicle to amplify their commitment to self-edification. In other words, the Satanic emphasis on personal power and self-preservation may be viewed as an extreme yet logical extension of the "thinking straight" theme, which was so popular throughout the 1980s. Moreover, as the straightedge subculture took on a more militant ethos into the 1990s, it is also logical that discontent with mainstream society was repackaged into a more extreme and reactionary format.

### Summary

My analysis of the straightedge music genre and scene provides insight into several cultural transitions or fluctuations endured by the subculture since the early 1980s. It is clear that straightedge is a phenomenon that has undergone change since its initial emergence. While some common themes persist over time, the nature of its boundaries has changed, sometimes in ways that could never have been predicted. Some of these changes are fairly obvious to insiders and observers of the straightedge phenomenon, whereas others are likely more difficult to detect at first glance.

In particular, this chapter identifies the following changes and processes at work within the straightedge subculture: (1) The concept of straightedge first emerged amidst the Washington, D.C., punk rock scene and stems specifically from songs written by Ian MacKaye of Minor Threat; (2) The early straightedge cultural ethos emphasized such themes as the importance of unity, opposition to substance use, and the value of being mentally and physically strong; (3) A distinctly identifiable straightedge music scene did not appear until the mid-1980s, led mainly by straightedge bands from New York; (4) During the later 1980s, straightedge opposition to substance use became more militant in nature, and animal rights emerged as an issue of concern; (5) During the late 1980s, the subculture began to experience some internal tension in reaction to perceived defectors as well as others who were seemed lacking in commitment; (6) New factions or iterations of straightedge culture began to emerge in the early 1990s, including (but not necessarily limited to) hardline and Krishna-core.

Having made these assertions about changes in the straightedge subculture, I must emphasize that I do not intend this as an exhaustive history. Indeed, there may be other broad and localized trends occurring since the early

1980s that warrant attention in future research. Having discussed several broad structural trends, I also do not wish to homogenize the identities of people who define themselves as straightedge. Indeed, just because hardline emerged as a powerful theme during the early 1990s does not mean that all or even most straightedge people of that era defined themselves as such. Hardline, as well as the other themes I've discussed, became elements of the straightedge frame of reference. But, as I discuss in subsequent chapters, a frame of reference is a socially constructed phenomenon that individuals differently perceive, adopt, and refer to in constructing a straightedge identity (or some variant thereof).

# 4 (Re)Negotiating a Straightedge Identity

## Identity in Subcultures Literature

**B**efore the late 1980s, subculture studies and theories only infrequently broached issues of identity among individual members of any given subculture. Instead, research focused almost exclusively on the cultural commonalities (i.e., norms, values, and beliefs commonly recognized by subculture members) that seemed to define the general character of the subculture and supposedly bind its members together (see, for example, Levine and Stumpf 1983). Embedded in this past research and theory is the latent assumption that individual members of a subculture share a highly similar identity that can be deduced simply by looking at its broad cultural parameters (e.g., Suall and Lowe 1988). Subcultural strain perspectives, for example, generally imply that the identities of individual subculture members get coerced and determined into relative homogeneity when they encounter a preexisting frame of reference (e.g., Cohen 1955). Later studies, inspired by early iterations of the more critical Birmingham perspective, are often equally as problematic insofar as they imply a homogeneity of subcultural identity stemming from the common class positions and experiences of subculture members (e.g., Clarke et al. 1976). Fortunately, recent research and theory, emerging largely from both a more contemporary Birmingham perspective (which places a heavier emphasis on interpreting individual voices) and the contemporary postmodern academic ethos (which emphasizes complexity), is making a much-needed departure from past implications of the homogeneity of subculture identity (e.g., Kearney 1998).

Contemporary subcultures research continues correctly to suggest that any given youth subculture is bound globally or generally by a set of cultural commonalities, including norms, values, and beliefs. Contemporary research, however, also explores the crucial fact that individual members of the subculture may differently understand, affiliate with, and internalize the same cultural commonalities, thereby respectively forming at least partially distinct identities.

Studies of punk subculture suggest that punks recognize common subcultural referents, and that they often also share an image of the punk ideal type (see Andes 1998; Fox 1987; Levine and Stumpf 1983). In other words, punks are conscious of a general set of parameters, or frame of reference, for punk culture and identity. Nonetheless, as studies further illustrate, the punk subculture is characterized by a high level of internal variation.

Illustrating such variation, Baron (1989) finds that the punk theme of resistance to mainstream society gets internalized and acted out by individual punks in different ways and with different levels of commitment and intensity. Similarly, in his well-known analysis of punk subculture, *Sub-*

# (Re)Negotiating a Straightedge Identity

*culture: The Meaning of Style,* Hebdige (1979) illustrates how shared class-based experiences allowed the British punk subculture to hang together, yet he also suggests that individual punks may encode the idiosyncrasies of their subjective life experiences into their own variations on punk style. Numerous other studies further suggest a high level of variation between the identities of members of a given subculture (see Bennet 1999; Fox 1987; Kearny 1998; Widdicombe and Wooffitt 1990; Young and Craig 1997). Indeed, in their study of Canadian skinheads, Young and Craig (1997, 175) find that "the skinhead subculture is both complex and multi-dimensional and it accommodates, albeit in often contradictory ways, a range of behavioral and ideological opportunities for its members." According to Young and Craig (1997), therefore, while skinheads may share some level of common or group identity, each individual may formulate a personal identity that reflects her or his subjective stance on the meanings of skinhead.

Thus, it is remiss of subculture researchers to stop short at merely delineating a set of overarching norms, values, and beliefs, which apparently cement a subculture together. Insofar as it leads to implications of identity homogeneity, it is even more problematic for researchers to simply deduce, from these broad cultural parameters, claims about the identities of individual subculture members. Indeed, if one were to examine a cross-section of a subculture at any particular time, rather than observing homogeneity of subcultural identity, researchers will find that the respective identities of its members are, in important ways, qualitatively different as well as differently salient. This framework serves as a conceptual guide for the present chapter, which explores the complexity of straightedge identity.

## Identity and Straightedge Lifestyle Tenets

Like all contemporary youth subcultures, straightedge can be distinguished by an overarching set of cultural parameters, recognized by all self-professed members of the subculture. As the reader is aware, straightedgers are known for their committed opposition to drugs, alcohol, and promiscuous/casual sex (Haenfler 2004; Irwin 1999; Lahickey 1997; Williams 2003; Wood 2003). Confirming the prominence of these lifestyle tenets in their culture and identity, every straightedger that I interviewed claimed to reject drugs, alcohol, and what they perceived as unhealthy forms of promiscuous or casual sexuality. Most seem to perceive these activities as symptomatic of personal weakness and to express a desire to always maintain control of their mental and physical faculties. However, while straightedgers consistently seem to base their respective identities upon universally recognized lifestyle tenets, interview data reveals that individuals often hold very different understandings of the meanings of those tenets and their role in defining an authentic straightedge identity.

One such difference involves the amount of flexibility that individual straightedgers allow within traditional lifestyle parameters. Reflecting a typical rigid stance, many straightedgers describe the stereotypical lifestyle tenets as a set of rules that one must strictly follow in order to legitimately claim a straightedge identity. Eighteen-year-old Alan

## (Re)Negotiating a Straightedge Identity

typified this position when he explained that individuals may legitimately claim a straightedge identity only when they have shown that they are "true": "Being true is following the basic, quote unquote, rules of not drinking, not smoking, not doing drugs, and no promiscuous sexual activity. Don't smoke, don't drink, don't fuck. Those are the rules. If you don't want to follow the rules, then unclaim."

Other straightedgers, however, embrace a more flexible set of lifestyle tenets. Rather than construing their identity as contingent on following rules, these straightedgers regard the typical "straightedge rules" merely as a broad and highly flexible guide embodying the straightedge perspective. Jason explains:

> I don't like it when people view it as kind of a set of rules, you know, where you have to do A, B, and C. I don't think that's what it's all about. . . . It's not like it comes with an instruction manual that tells you, "Okay, here's the steps." I think it's basically . . . living your life the best way you know how. And, trying to achieve your goals and not let[ting] anything get in your way. . . . It's just a way of thinking about things and viewing things.

Even Ian MacKaye never intended his straightedge lyrics as a formal set of rules: "You have to be interpretive of these things. You just can't look at the words and go, 'Oh, we're not supposed to do this, this, or this.' " Thus, a number of straightedgers reject the idea that their identity hinges upon strictly following a predetermined set of lifestyle parameters or rules. Instead, these straightedgers suggest that the lifestyle tenets serve only as a general guideline that may be reinterpreted or even only partially adopted.

In addition to differing in terms of the perceived importance of following rules, straightedgers often do not agree about the meaning of the rules. In other words, even though every straightedger that I interviewed claimed not to drink, do drugs, or engage in promiscuous/casual sex, their understanding varied as to exactly what these acts entail. One point of divergence was the characterization of casual/promiscuous sex. Alan exemplified a typical straightedge stance when he explained that he is very serious about his opposition to it: "I believe in total monogamy. I don't believe in sex before marriage." Alan told me that he knows some unmarried straightedge individuals who are sexually active; in his opinion, they are not authentic straightedgers. Conversely, Allison outlines a relatively different opinion of sexuality and straightedge identity:

> I feel a lot of the straightedge rules have been shaped
> predominantly by men participants in the scene. . . . In
> our culture, we encourage men to display their
> masculinity and their cultural dominance or power
> through sexuality, where my understanding is that
> women have been acculturated to repress [their
> sexuality]. . . . Men specifically, I think, are bombarded
> with the encouragement to be sexually aggressive and
> promiscuous. . . . For a man, perhaps not engaging in
> sexual activity, maybe that's a liberating experience. . . .
> I think it's a different experience for a woman. Part of my
> experience as a woman has been coming to terms with

sexuality, and requestioning sexuality, and trying to re-evaluate and come to terms with a sexuality and identity that is good for me, that is constructive for me, is healthy for me, and is a liberating practice for me.

While Allison's view certainly does not necessitate engaging in promiscuous sexual activity, it does allow for the possibility of sexual activity outside of marriage. What the reader might observe, however, is that Allison's goal of critically evaluating her sexuality has the potential to clash outright with Alan's emphasis on the importance of monogamy and abstinence from premarital sex. Consequently, we see two self-identified straightedge individuals espousing very different views on the same lifestyle tenet.

A similar disjunction arises over what actually constitutes drug use. Some straightedgers claim that, in addition to abstaining from alcohol and illicit drugs, they abstain from legal and nonpsychoactive drugs, such as caffeine. Vessel, for example, says: "To me, it's doing no drugs at all, including no cigarettes, or no alcohol, [or] no caffeine." Benjamin does not agree that caffeine is a problematic substance to be avoided. However, he does explain that caffeine has become a problematic substance for him personally:

I've kind of taken a long time assessing my life, what substances influence me, and a big substance that influences me is Coca-Cola. . . . A lot of caffeine in it, a lot of sugar, and it totally affects my mood. . . . If I have, like, a can of Coke in a day, I crave it the next day, and the day after, and the day after that. . . . I know that the caffeine and the sugar are causing my body to want to buy it. And that makes me feel a little bit weaker, you know, a little bit not in control of myself.

Not all straightedgers agree that caffeine is problematic. Indeed, Ian MacKaye recalls his reaction on being confronted by a disgruntled straightedge onlooker as he was drinking an iced tea: "I had this one kid say to me, 'I can't believe you're drinking iced tea.' I was like, 'What?' And he said, 'In my book, caffeine is a drug.' I said, 'Fuck you' " (Ian MacKaye, quoted in Lahickey 1997). Thus, while all straightedge individuals apparently agree that their identity involves opposition to drugs, there is substantial intragroup conflict about what susbtances are properly classified as drugs.

Some of the staunchest intrasubcultural dissent stems from disagreements about vegetarianism and veganism. While it was not originally associated with straightedge, it appears that vegetarianism and veganism spread across the culture with surprising momentum beginning in the late 1980s. Ian MacKaye himself became vegetarian several years after coining the straightedge concept: "I wasn't a vegetarian until 1984 or so. . . . I think that vegetarianism was a logical step for straightedge. For me, it was logical. To me, it's a process. The idea of my life, of the process, that is, is reexamining things given to me and seeing if they work and constantly working to make myself better—do a better job in the world. So, it just seemed to make sense" (Ian MacKaye, quoted in Lahickey 1997, 103). Here MacKaye does not articulate vegetarianism as a straightedge rule, yet he does imply that it is a natural lifestyle progression given his own perceptions of the meaning of straightedge. In contrast, others strongly claim that vegetarianism and veganism can not assume a legitimate place. Jack, a singer for Slapshot, says: "When I got into it, it was no smoking, no drinking, no doing drugs." He further explains that, in his opinion, the introduction of veganism and vegetarianism has convoluted and distorted the original meaning of the concept.

In sum, in straightedge as in other subcultural groups, an overarching set of cultural parameters appears to act as a sort of cement for the subculture. All of the individuals that I interviewed identified opposition to alcohol, illicit substances, and promiscuous sexual activity as fundamental aspects of their respective straightedge identities. Many interviewees further identified vegetarianism or veganism as an additional important component. Given the common acceptance of these lifestyle tenets, it might be easy for observers to assume that straightedge identity is a roughly monolithic and homogenous phenomenon among all self-identified members of the subculture. However, interview data contradicts this assumption, revealing instead that straightedgers may hold very different perceptions, experiences, and understandings of cultural parameters and of what constitutes an authentic straightedge identity. Consequently, we see different individuals claiming distinct straightedge identities.

## Identity and Gendered Experiences

Similar to other contemporary youth subcultures, many aspects of the straightedge subculture are embedded with a latent male-oriented bias. The subculture does indeed appear to be populated mostly by males, with an even greater disproportion represented among the genre's prominent bands. Subtle discursive examples of gender bias may involve instances of male straightedgers unwittingly making male-centered references to the subculture as a sort of brotherhood, a theme common among both straightedge music lyrics and comments of males interviewed for this study. Additionally, and unfortunately, more harmful examples of overt sexism occasionally can be found in straightedge culture. On one Internet message board, I observed a discussion about straightedge music gigs in which a male expressed his dislike for female straightedgers by writing: "No clit in the pit." Presumably "clit" is meant as a reference to the female clitoris, and "pit" is meant as a reference to the mosh pits that invariably form at straightedge music gigs.

Gender bias and sexism directly impact the experiences and the identities of many straightedge women. For instance, Janine described scenarios of feeling socially excluded, especially at straightedge music gigs: "I definitely got ignored by a lot of the guys. Like, I wasn't taken seriously sometimes just because, I don't know, I guess it was just because I was a girl and they thought that, you know, girls don't count or whatever. . . . I think they wanted it to be like an all-guy bonding thing."

Allison is another straightedge woman who describes a similar sort of social exclusion: "In the scene, I've often felt invisible, and I think I can attribute that to people treating me a certain way because of my gender. For example, I'll show up at a show with, like, four of my guy friends, and they'll be talking to someone in a band who they just met, and the person will be introduced to all the guys but not me."

Other women, such as Dawn, refuse to remain invisible in the scene. As Dawn explained, her unwillingness to conform to straightedge gender expectations led to a low-key yet consistent animosity between her and her male counterparts:

> If you were the sort of girl that they wanted to go out with, then you were accepted. But, even then, they thought you were going to hold their coats at the back. . . . If you were up there dancing and stuff, like they almost thought it was really gross, like icky, like you were a brute or something. . . . So, I wasn't the girl that they wanted to go out with, and they felt kind of threatened because I knew just as much about hardcore as they did. You know, I knew the bands, and I went to the shows, and I sang along, and in a way they found that very threatening, I think.

When I asked about the source of gender bias and the social exclusion of women, Allison suggested that these issues stem from stereotypical conceptions of a female's role within the straightedge music scene: "I think what often goes assumed is that a girl who's there at a show is there because her boyfriend's into it. Her boyfriend's in a band or she wants to meet guys, and I think that's a really big misconception." Allison further explained that biased conceptions of women have made it difficult to garner recognition as a legitimate and authentic actor within the straightedge music scene: "It has definitely forced me to extend myself where I think guys don't have to go a lot of the time. It's made me have to be a lot louder in my voice." To this end, Allison and her friends have formed a band with music geared towards the female experience in the hardcore/ straightedge music scene: "We started a band because we felt that, literally, our voices weren't heard in the scene. Our female voices in general, not just OUR female voices. But female voices weren't or haven't been equally represented. . . . and so we started a band. All we're talking about in our music are the experiences of being female in the scene."

In sum, straightedge women who do encounter sexism, gender bias, and social exclusion are relegated to a paradoxical situation. Similar to their male counterparts, they develop a straightedge identity as a way of resisting or reacting to certain norms and values in the mainstream society. Unlike their male counterparts, however, that identity often gets challenged internally both by other straightedgers and by a male-oriented subcultural ethos in general. Consequently, some straightedge women may feel that they must work doubly hard, relative to their male counterparts, to gain acceptance and to maintain a legitimate identity.

## Identity and Social Networks

Subculture theories often imply that an individual's subcultural identity forms through interaction with like-minded others. Even early strain theories, which get criticized for

## (Re)Negotiating a Straightedge Identity

being overly deterministic and static, imply that identity emerges through interactive processes of "mutual conversion" (Cohen 1955) or a "conversation of gestures" (Cloward and Ohlin 1960) between subculture and prospective members. Such theories find support in comments made by the straightedgers that I interviewed, many of whom claimed to have been involved, at one time or another, with relatively dense localized networks of individuals who were influential in shaping and maintaining their own straightedge identity:

> We would go to the local store here and go, "Have you got Minor Threat records?" And they're like, "Yeah, we sure do." And we would buy it and there would be two other kids buying it, and we'd look at them and go, "How you doing?" And then we'd start chatting, and they would go, "Hey, you going to see this band down at the [hall] this weekend?" So, we'd go to the show and you'd meet thirty other like-minded people.

Many straightedge individuals describe such local social networks as an important source of friendship and support. Janine tells me: "I'll just meet someone who happens to also be straightedge, and that's a lot of support. . . . Someone who's straightedge can relate to what I'm going through." Similarly describing his straightedge friendships as a source of support, Thomas says: "I have a few really good friends who are straightedge, and my girlfriend is straightedge. So, that's a very, very good thing." Thus, for some straightedge individuals, local social networks are crucial in constructing and maintaining an identity and a commitment to the lifestyle. Indeed, in the midst of a relatively antagonistic mainstream teen culture, networks facilitate for some individuals a sense of both belonging and security.

Interestingly, other straightedgers claim not to be part of any local or "real world" social networks, but instead maintain a strong sense of identity via alternate modes of networking over the Internet. Alan, for example, says: "Name a straightedge site on the Web and I have probably been there. I am all about learning about how other straightedge kids live, what their true beliefs are." Also, Sarah is not networked with a sizeable local group of straightedgers, but she interacts with others on Internet message boards: "It's basically a glorified chat room. . . . They just post messages and other people respond to them, and you can post pictures or Web sites and things." Still other straightedgers claim to maintain their identity in the absence of any sort of network, whether it be online or in the real world. Neil explained that he is not friends with any other straightedge individuals and does not know of any others in his community, nor is he networked with straightedgers on the Internet. He heard about straightedge through music and made a commitment to the subculture in isolation from other members.

In sum, face-to-face social interactions obviously are important to at least some self-professed straightedge individuals. The straightedge case suggests, however, that face-to-face interaction is not necessary for people to affiliate or identify themselves with a subculture. On the contrary, it appears that the only really necessary component for self

## (Re)Negotiating a Straightedge Identity

identification is access to some form of conduit into the sub-culture's frame of reference. This conduit may emerge in the form of an individual, or it may take the form of a song or an Internet Web site. These latter sorts of solitary affiliation processes are likely to become more prominent as new media and technologies increase the access to subcultural frames of reference for socially isolated individuals.

### Identity and (In)Tolerance

The present study disconfirms media stereotypes of straight-edge as a predominantly violent subculture. Of the twenty individuals that I interviewed, only Alan currently expresses limited support for violence against nonstraightedge individuals. Even then, he suggests that he uses violence only against "people who are mocking the X." To illustrate what he means by this, Alan outlined the following scenario:

> Say I am at a party. Someone sitting next to me is smoking a cig. I will either: one, move, or two, ask him to put it out. Then, one of two things are gonna happen. Either they're gonna move and blow opposite to me. Or, they're gonna blow it back in my face. . . . Of course, it's automatically gonna set me off. He knew what I was, he knew I disagreed with it, yet he blew it back in my face. And, nine times out of ten, I'm gonna break his nose. . . . Usually the fighting always ends up because it's the respect issue. . . . That's the reason I fight now. . . . It's just because they are disrespecting my life, right in my face.

# Straightedge Youth

Here, Alan elaborates a vocabulary of motive that articulates his use of violence as a legitimate defense in situations of provocation. Indeed, drawing upon the phenomenological ideas of Jack Katz (1988), one could argue that Alan's use of violence is a defensive act of transcending a perceived threat to his moral existence. In other words, Alan's use of limited violence constitutes a verification and affirmation of his straightedge self-identity.

Every other straightedger that I interviewed claimed to oppose violence, and some people even questioned the authenticity of straightedgers who do use violence. Indeed, far from advocating a violent stance, many of the individuals that I interviewed claimed a high level of tolerance for people who do not live a similar lifestyle. Leo, for example, explained to me: "People know that I don't like smoking, and people know that I don't like drinking. But at the same time, if someone's like, 'Oh, I'm having a party,' I'm still going to go there. I know that people are going to drink there. . . . I accept it as long as people understand my reasons for not doing it."

In this miniscule interaction, Leo is constrained to explore the boundaries of his straightedge identity, and he may choose actions that support and affirm it. Indeed, Leo further explained that he feels a sense of pride, satisfaction, and strength in adhering to his straightedge convictions when his friends and acquaintances bring him into situations involving alcohol.

Jason, another straightedger, explained to me that when he was younger he experienced difficulties tolerating drinkers and drug users. However, as he grew up, he developed a high level of tolerance for individuals who do not live a straightedge lifestyle: "Just because someone has a drink, or smokes a cigarette, they're not a bad person. It's not preventing them from living their life." Similarly, Jeff claims: "Most of my friends are that way [not straightedge]. . . . I don't think somebody is, you know, a shit of a person just because they may have a beer or a glass of wine with dinner every so often. . . . Each person has good things about them that are worthwhile, whether they believe exactly the way I do or not."

Here, in the comments of Jeff and Jason, we see a sort of maturation effect. As straightedgers encounter situations that challenge or contradict the past meanings that they attach to straightedge-relevant social objects, these individuals modify meanings and consequently experience a transition in their own sense of identity.

Thus, straightedge interactions with nonstraightedgers span a continuum, ranging from rare instances of extreme violence to varying levels of tolerance. Regardless of the nature of the interaction, straightedge individuals are forced to explore and potentially modify their identity when interacting with those who do not subscribe to the culture. Consequently, we can envision subcultural identity as a condition in perpetual flux, resulting from the individual accumulating new experiences.

## Managing Competing Identities

When examining subcultural groups, especially ones with apparently distinct ideological and normative boundaries, researchers should be cautious about inadvertently essentializing the people being studied. In other words, researchers should not assume that a self-identified straightedger has an identity that is uniformly and exclusively straightedge in nature. Interview data suggest quite the opposite. Straightedge individuals, to varying degrees, balance their identity with other important and potentially competing identities.

Suggesting that subcultural identities are not mutually exclusive, some straightedgers identified themselves with more than one group concurrently. Dawn, for example, claims that she is both a straightedger and skinhead (of a nonracist variety). For her, there is little difficulty accommodating both identities. Straightedge enables her to sustain a sense of personal health and mental well-being. Her attraction to the skinhead phenomenon, in contrast, stems from an understanding and pride that she feels about her perceived socioeconomic class background: "To me it was definitely like this whole blue-collar pride thing. This whole, like, you know, work ethic that was instilled in me by my father, and a way to kick pride in the face of people who thought I was white trash completely." In contrast to Dawn's experience of easily accommodating both straightedge and skinhead identities, Benjamin, another straightedger and former SHARP skinhead (Skinheads Against Racial Prejudice), explains that he was unable to achieve such a balance: "The whole subculture's so restricting and so confining. You have to dress in a very, very specific style. You have to listen to sort of only very specific kinds of music, you have to drink beer, you have to love soccer. And that, aside from the class identity, a lot wasn't really resonating for me. . . . I was straightedge before I was skinhead, so drinking was out of the question."

Here we see that Benjamin's identity as straightedge came into direct conflict with his perception of informal skinhead expectations about drinking beer.

Apart from maintaining and balancing different subcultural identities, many of the individuals explained that they integrated or concurrently maintained political activism with their straightedge identities. Indeed, confirming the distinctly political and public quality that veganism holds for many straightedge individuals, a number of people claimed to be politically active on the basis of their vegan beliefs. Derek explains that he founded an animal rights group on his college campus: "I'm a member of PETA and the National Anti-Vivisection Society, but they don't really do too much, and there was no animal rights club here. So my friends and I took the stand, and we started an animal rights club." Other examples of straightedgers' political activism appear in the form of involving themselves with formal antiracist organizations. Leo claims to be active in an organization known as Anti-Racist Action (ARA):

> Where I live right now, there are no ARA chapters,
> which automatically means that I have not been
> physically involved. I have been online involved. . . .
> people from all over the world that support ARA go
> there and just talk to other people online. I am actually
> an operator there, which means that I am in charge of
> kind of the channel's safety and security. . . . For me

> going to ARA is a way to learn more, become a better
> person, and also to help other people. . . . I've met lots
> of straightedge people online, which is kind of
> interesting because I never equated the anti-racist
> movement with straightedge.

Despite Leo's surprise about meeting other straightedgers
through ARA, a number of other individuals that I interviewed also involve themselves with Anti-Racist Action.

It is clear that straightedgers may concurrently maintain
other prominent identities. This multiplexity of identity
should cause researchers to exercise caution when discussing the cultural and identity boundaries of any given
subculture. As opposed to essentializing the identities of individual subculture members, researchers should view affiliation as a process of identity salience. Straightedge
individuals may maintain different cultural affiliations, each
one assuming a more or less salient position in the individual's identity repertoire at different points in time.

### Identity Transition

Over the course of my discussions with straightedge individuals, a remarkable dichotomy emerged in their descriptions of their pre-straightedge identities and lifestyles. Some
described their current identity as continuous or compatible
with their former identity. These people explained that they
had always lived a straightedge-compatible lifestyle, dis-
covering relatively suddenly that they had (in their opinion)
been straightedge all along. Derek is a case in point. He ex-

plained to me that he never had used alcohol or drugs even before calling himself straightedge, and that straightedge simply validated a lifestyle he already was living: "I didn't do drugs or anything before I found out about straightedge." Sarah similarly claims that when she first discovered straightedge, it seemed a natural fit with her lifestyle: "I found out that it was this drug-free subculture, and it sort of fit with me because I was raised in a drug-free, alcohol-free environment my whole life. . . . I had to change nothing at all because I'd never been into any of it, and that's why it seemed like such a natural thing to do."

In contrast, others described straightedge as a disjunction from their former identity. These people often described prior histories of drinking and drug use, and spoke about becoming straightedge for the purpose of achieving a healthier and more productive lifestyle. Claiming to have had a problem with alcohol, Allison said: "I used to do drugs and drink and smoke cigarettes. I struggled with addiction and alcoholism when I was from the ages of, like, sixteen to about seventeen." Dawn explains that she first became straightedge in the mid-1980s, when she was fourteen years old, but that she developed a drug addiction during the early 1990s. She received treatment and again defined herself as straightedge in about 1993. Dawn further explains that her second claim to straightedge was instrumental in nature: "The goal for me was to rebuild a healthy life, and to maintain it, and to accomplish the things that I wanted to accomplish that I wouldn't be able to do [if I was using drugs or alcohol]."

Other straightedgers explained that, although they

never had involved themselves with alcohol and drugs, their decision to live the lifestyle stems at least partially from their observations of the negative impact drugs and alcohol have on people close to them. Alan explains that he finds conviction in his choice to be straightedge having watched his grandmother die from smoking-related lung cancer, and also having observed the sorts of problems that alcohol causes in his brother's life. Jason's words also illustrate this theme when he explains that his decision to live a straight-edge lifestyle stems at least partially from his observations of the effect that alcoholism had on his father: "He had a big alcohol and drug problem, and I guess I kind of saw myself starting down that same path, and I just told myself this isn't what I want out of life."

Thus, straightedge individuals seem to report either a continuity or disjunction between their current and former identities. For some, straightedge represents a conscious radical departure from a former lifestyle and a drastic rearticulation of a former identity. These people often de-scribe straightedge as both a means to a healthy sense of self and a means to achieving goals that might be impeded by drug and alcohol use. Others form a straightedge identity as a validation and continuation of a former identity. In a sense, these individuals feel that they have been straight-edge all along. Still others form the identity at least partially in response to their perceptions of the harm that drugs and alcohol cause to people in their primary social networks.

Regardless of the continuity or disjunction of pre-straightedge and straightedge identity, many individuals ex-perience a substantial amount of identity fluctuation

# (Re)Negotiating a Straightedge Identity

throughout their affiliation with straightedge. Indeed, many self-professed straightedge individuals explained that the concept resonated differently for them throughout their life history. Jack, who was involved in straightedge during its earliest years, explains: "I mean, I'm thirty-seven now, and I mean as far as calling myself straightedge? No, probably not, because the general spirit of it has changed over the years. . . . Calling myself straightedge in public, people would get the wrong idea. . . . It just becomes so cloudy and convoluted that no one really knows what it is anymore."

Similarly, while he does not reject the straightedge label, Jason claims that the concept does not assume the same sort of master status in his persona as it once did: "A lot of times I don't really even call myself straightedge. . . . Like I said, I'm not as vocal about it."

Other individuals experience a much more significant and abrupt transition out of their straightedge identity as they gain new experiences not easily accommodated within the parameters of the culture or what the individual perceives as an authentic identity. Pete drifted away from straightedge while on tour with his band, Verbal Assault:

> By the time we went to Europe for the second time I still didn't drink, but I realized that I felt that I kind of missed out a lot of times that people in the band had during the first trip. . . . I realized that I would rather stay up until six in the morning drinking with a band from Norway, and talking with them, than go to bed early. . . . What I'm saying is that by 1989, I found that I would much rather be involved with experiences around me than

stick to an idea or a kind of philosophy I had in the back
of my mind. (Pete, quoted in Lahickey 1997, 198)

Pete reached a point where straightedge no longer fit or
made sense in relation to other facets of his life, and so the
salience of his straightedge identity waned and ultimately
disappeared as a manifest element of his identity repertoire.

Thus, subcultural identity is not a condition that necessarily is either present or absent. It is a constantly iterating
condition that ebbs, flows, wanes, or rejuvenates in a diachronic fashion. In other words, identity is fluid over time
and space. The salience, priority, and meaning of an individual's straightedge identity transforms in response to interactions with his or her social world.

## Summary

Consistent with studies of other subcultural groups, the
straightedge case suggests that subculture is generally
bound by a frame of reference, or a set of cultural commonalities, that most members use as a guide for forming and
maintaining a subcultural identity. Individual straightedgers, however, may hold respectively different understandings of straightedge norms and values; they may
selectively and differentially internalize those norms and
values and hence form respectively different identities. Indeed, if we were to examine a point-in-time cross-section of
the straightedge subculture, we would observe that individuals' identities are respectively different. Additionally, if we
were to track any single individual's straightedge identity

over time and space, we would observe that her or his individual identity becomes both qualitatively different as well as differently salient. Thus, this study confirms a simple yet crucial fact that subcultural identity is complex and diachronic in nature, as opposed to homogenous and static. Moreover, this study illustrates that subcultural identity is not mutually exclusive of other identities.

# 5 Straightedge in Social and Historical Context

## The Importance of Social and Historical Context

**A** common problem among many contemporary studies of youth culture is the tendency for the researcher to extract and isolate the subcultural phenomenon from the social and historical context in which it emerges, changes, and even declines. Recent studies of the American skinhead phenomenon, for example, in their attempts to document what skinheads say, think, and do, overlook or exclude the social and historical contexts that likely inform skinhead norms and values over time (see Baron 1997; Young and Craig 1997; Hamm 1993). Consequently, such studies inadvertently suggest that the content of the subculture at the time of the research reflects the content of the subculture historically.

Not all subculture studies suffer this deficiency. On the contrary, writers adhering to the perspectives of the Birmingham School of Cultural Studies construe youth cultures and subcultures as phenomena that ebb, flow, and change with historical shifts in the structure of society. Regarding the rise of punk culture during the mid 1970s in Britain, observers suggest that punk embodied something of a collectively perceived and experienced contradiction between ideology and reality. In particular, observers generally imply that punk embodied the conflict between the ideal of consumerism and the reality of rising unemployment and economic austerity among British youth. Thus, in something of a dramatization of this conflicting state of affairs, British punks in the late 1970s allegedly championed all things that, from the perspective of mainstream culture, were offensive, perverse, chaotic, and threatening, and they defined their subcultural space through symbols of nihilism, anarchy, and violence (Brake 1993; Hamm 1993, 29; Hebdige 1979, 106–7).

The reader will recall my earlier discussion of the theoretical contributions of David Matza, who makes the simple yet crucial observation that the social spaces inhabited by youth are encircled and permeated by conventional cultural agents. Thus, by definition, all subcultures at least partially are informed by the encircling and permeating social context. It is naïve to assume that any novel cultural phenomenon emerges in a social vacuum, and the straightedge youth culture is no exception. Indeed, from my analysis of interview data, several crucial and recurring themes emerged to suggest that straightedge cultural boundaries get constructed often in relation to external cultural agents and environments.

## Early Connections Between Straightedge and Punk

By all accounts, the straightedge phenomenon emerged and gained momentum within the American punk scene, and interview evidence suggests that straightedge and non-straightedge individuals for awhile maintained at least a tenuous and loose alliance within the punk scene. According to Dan, hardcore punk gigs in Boston during the early 1980s involved a cross section of the entire local punk subculture. Moreover, as Dan explains, different types of punks maintained a relatively peaceful coexistence: "We tended to consider everybody that went to these shows hardcore, whether they were straightedge or not. . . . The overview was that we were all different, no matter what kind of school we were coming from. Whether it was crusty punks, or mohawk guys, or straightedge, or just hardcore no-hair kids, that we were all part of something that was unique. It's kind of like factions within the church, I guess."

Other straightedgers spoke also about the early intrascene alliance between punks and straightedgers. Jason, in particular, elaborates a sentiment that strongly parallels Dan's view of punk/straightedge coexistence: "I don't know if it was just my point of view, but back then it seemed like everybody went to every type of show. Whether it was a straightedge show, whether the band was straightedge or not, you would have punks there, you would have straightedge kids there."

Jason further elaborates his perception that contemporary straightedge individuals are not particularly likely to affiliate with the broader punk scene: "Now it seems very splintered. It seems like straightedgers will only go to a show if it's a straightedge band, you know what I mean? And I think that's a problem. I think a lot of the kids are very closed-minded now."

## Social and Historical Context

Dawn explained her perceptions of the mid—1980s Connecticut punk/hardcore scene as a mixed subcultural environment: "When I first got into hardcore back in, like, '86, the scene that I was around was more of a hybrid scene. There were a lot of, like, punks, and straightedge kids, and hardcore kids, and skinheads, and it was all kind of one big scene."

While most observers of the early straightedge phenomenon identify a similar sort of united scene alliance, it appears that unity between straightedge and nonstraightedge punks was relatively short lived. Dawn explained her perceptions of a rift emerging in the New York punk scene beginning in the late 1980s: "You know, there started to be a divide in the scene between straightedge, and between hardcore and punk. . . . Around '88 or so, you started seeing, like, a real big divide in the scene. You started seeing straightedge bands playing together and never playing with punk bands. . . . You know, straightedge and a punk band together and everyone would stay outside during the punk band."

Confirming Dawn's perceptions, Jeff also remembers the emergence of a distinct straightedge music scene during the late 1980s: "The late eighties is where the whole hardcore and straightedge thing, the punk and straightedge thing sort of separated. . . . It's really tough to say where it started, whether it was the punks separating from straightedge kids or the straightedge kids not wanting to have anything to do with the punks."

# Straightedge Youth

## Straightedge as a Reaction to Punk Culture

Interview evidence suggests that the emerging rift in the late-1980s punk scene stems largely from cultural incompatibilities between straightedge and punk. Straightedge staked its own distinct claim to punk authenticity during the 1980s, and it did so in a way that drastically rearticulated and challenged typical meanings of punk. Ian MacKaye explained that the idea of straightedge did not generally encounter a warm reception within the punk scene, and that the straight punks of the Washington, D.C., area in the early 1980s were not fully accepted by many older, long-term punks:

> You've got to remember that the older punk scene was really fashion-based, and kind of druggy. There was, like, Johnny Thunders, the Dolls, the Sex Pistols. . . . It was really druggy, and kind of, like, snobby, and arty. And we were saying, look, we were punk rockers but we were, like, hardcore punk rockers. We're young. We were being called teeny punks. That's what they referred to us as in D.C. all the time. And it made us mad, because we felt like we saw punk rock as sort of, like, this safe haven for deviance. We felt as if we were deviant. I mean, there was all these other people who were challenging all these conventions. Sexual conventions, political conventions, sociological conventions, philosophical conventions—every kind of convention, musical and artistic, all this stuff. There were people who were challenging these conventions and so were we. We were challenging social

conventions, too. And we felt like we belonged there and that we should be respected. But what we ran into was a real snobbery with a lot of the older punks who felt like that either we were some weird fundamentalist Christian kids, or that we were just stupid, violent kind of kids.

MacKaye explains that punk largely was about challenging social conventions, and he further claims that he and his friends were resisting the social and cultural conventions that encourage drinking and drug use by teens. Therefore, "straight punks," because of their rebellion against mainstream conventions, deserved a legitimate place in the broader punk scene.

MacKaye further distinguished straightedge from the rest of the punk scene by arguing that the punks' use of drugs and alcohol does not constitute a true form of rebellion: "It just seemed like a strange form of rebellion, and one that I still think is. I still [consider] . . . smoking, and drinking, and even drug-taking . . . state-sponsored rebellion." MacKaye believes that his song "Straight Edge" resonated so strongly among the various American punk scenes in the early 1980s precisely because so many self-professed punks rejected the nihilism characteristic of punk culture. He speculates that the straightedge concept embodied a crucial yet latent sentiment felt by a significant minority of punks in his local scene:

Ultimately, when it boils down to it, if there was some sense of competition at all, that I am not a junkie gives me somewhat of an edge. Whereas it is safe to argue that someone who is a junkie or an alcoholic is not entirely in control. They're somewhat at the mercy of their habit. So I tried to articulate in the song my ideas about it. The song ["Straight Edge"], really, it resonated with a lot of people—a lot more than I had ever imagined. . . . I felt like the people really keyed on that song. They really looked in on it because I think there were a lot of punk rockers who were straight, who felt like, finally, here is someone who's straight.

Other individuals involved in the early straightedge scene confirmed MacKaye's speculations about discontent with the punk scene, especially the role of alcohol and drugs. According to Jeff, "I don't think that being punk includes, you know, hanging out at bars and drinking alcohol, you know, just like every other college kid and young adult does. You know, that's not what I consider to be punk at all. . . . But, I think anything you do to separate yourself from what goes on in mainstream society is punk. And, again, I think mainstream is definitely geared towards drugs and alcohol."

Reminiscing about the New York punk scene of the early—to mid-1980s, Porcell also expresses disdain for the proliferation of drugs and alcohol:

It was a very, very drug-oriented scene. . . . And I tell you, my early memories of going to CBGB's and, like, the hardcore scene, you're walking into the bathroom, and there's, like, six guys in there sniffing glue, and everyone is rocked out of their mind. People are just passed out in the corner. It was pretty horrible. Those early memories, they reinforced in me that this is a destructive thing, and this is horrible, and this has nothing to do with punk rock, or supposedly trying to go out and make a change in the world. . . . I was like, "This is ridiculous!" And I was even thinking, "How is this the alternative?" My whole life [when I was growing up], . . .on the weekend you go to a party, and people would get drunk, and they get in fights. Then you have the punk scene, which is supposed to be this big alternative, and what happens? People, like, go to shows, and they get drunk, and they get in fights on the weekend. It's totally ridiculous. It was white-bread suburban life in leather jackets and spike bracelets.

In sum, straightedge apparently assumes the position of being informed by the broader American punk cultural ethos while articulating a claim to punk authenticity that critiques and ultimately rejects that ethos. This process illustrates the central importance of latency in the initial generation of novel youth subcultures. Before McKaye's formal articulation of the straightedge concept, straightedge sentiments comprised a latent yet obviously present element of the American punk ethos. MacKaye's song ignited these latent sentiments, transforming them into a manifest concept. Once that happened, discontented punk rockers who were straight apprehended the concept and used it as a means of rearticulating the meaning of punk, of validating their own authenticity as punk rockers, and of challenging the authenticity of other punk rockers.

## Straightedge as a Reaction to Mainstream Teen Culture

Apart from emerging in reaction to elements of the punk subculture, straightedge also emerged in opposition to the drinking and drug use characteristic of mainstream teen culture. Many of the straightedgers that I interviewed stated that they perceive alcohol and drugs as pervasive and consistent elements of teen culture, elements that they didn't wish to incorporate into their own lives. Ian MacKaye, who went to high school during the late 1970s, explained that he could not relate, at the time, to his peers' drinking and drug use, and that he simply did not wish to participate:

> In the late seventies, I mean, everybody got high. I mean, in my high school, everybody got high or drank. . . . For me, it just seemed like a really stupid way to spend time. It just seemed like in the trajectory of life that, those years, it seemed such a waste of time to only think about medicating oneself. . . . In my first band that I was in [The Slinkees], we wrote a song called "Milk and Coke," which was probably the first sort of straightedge song. It went, "I drink milk, I drink milk, I drink milk, I drink milk/I don't care what people say, I drink milk for the vitamin A/I drink Coke, I drink Coke, I drink Coke, I drink Coke/I don't care what people say, I drink coke for the tooth decay." But the idea was we

**100**

didn't drink beer. It was silly, it was just kind of fun, it was not a big deal. But it was speaking directly to these high school kids.

For MacKaye, the very idea of straightedge emerged at least partially in reaction to his perceptions and experiences of drinking and drug use among his high school peers. Furthermore, his earliest elaborations of straightedge were attempts to validate and legitimize the deviant practices (at least among late 1970s youth culture) of *not* drinking and *not* using drugs.

Also commenting on the centrality of drinking and drug use in local teen culture, Jack explained: "Where I grew up—a lot of alcoholics, small town—really the only thing to do was you either have sex, or, you know, got shit-faced, or a combination of everything. There was a lot of drugs; it was mid—to late seventies." Vessel also perceived a proliferation of drinking and drug use among her teen peers, yet she links their substance use to broader societal expectations: "It kind of bothered me because I knew that they were intelligent people, but they were doing things like that just to fit in or because they thought it was cool. And I think they just thought it was cool because it's been pushed down their throats all their lives. It's kind of something that society tells people that it's a normal part of, like almost a rite of passage. Being a teenager is to drink and do drugs."

Many other straightedgers also identified an aversion to mainstream teen culture as an influential factor in becoming straightedge. Indeed, most explained that they simply could not identify with their peers' alcohol and drug use. Dan, for example, says:

> When we were kids, we saw all around us the kids in our town. . . . The older hippie kids would buy beer for the younger kids, and they would all hang out together and get drunk and get into trouble and that sort of thing, and we just thought that that wasn't a very good lifestyle. . . . We wanted to react differently, we didn't want to be part of this, so we even called ourselves "the new breed." You know, these two or three kids that weren't going to go down the hippie path, the substance-abuse path. You know, we shied away from everything that was related to that.

Another straightedger, Thomas, laments the fact that his college of choice ended up being "a big party school." According to Thomas, "It was mainly just a lot of drinking and smoking pot, and I just couldn't relate to any of those people." Similarly expressing disappointment, Ian MacKaye explains: "I guess at the time I felt that it was kind of dumb and I didn't have any patience for it. I was a skateboarder, so if I went to parties and if everyone was going to drink, I was like, 'fuck it, let's just go skating,' because it seemed like a much more interesting way to spend time."

Some people explained that their aversion to drinking and drugs left them feeling alienated or left out among their mainstream teen peers. For some of these individuals, the straightedge concept helped them to impute meaning and dignity to their lifestyle choices. Janine says: "It gave me a sense of belonging to something, instead of just this girl that doesn't do anything. Instead, I was this girl that doesn't do anything for a reason." Thomas described to me how he eventually began to feel embarrassed about not drinking and using drugs. For him, straightedge allowed him to deal with these negative feelings: "It was a way that people like me could actually feel proud of their choice instead of feeling like they're outside the normal and, you know, outcast. So, I started going around college, I was in a college full of potheads, and I started putting Xs on my hands. Nobody even knew what the hell I was doing, but I would happily tell them when they asked. It made me feel better about myself."

## Latent Cultural Support from the War on Drugs

Thus far, it is apparent that straightedge cultural boundaries, by way of reaction, garner latent support from both mainstream teen culture and punk subculture. These cultural phenomena embody certain ideals and normative practices that comprise the antithesis of straightedge and thereby serve as boundary signifiers. Additionally, however, the straightedge phenomenon likely received positive reinforcement from still other external cultural phenomena. Particularly striking is the coincidence in timing between the emergence and development of the straightedge subculture and the declaration and waging of a war on drugs by American politicians in the early 1980s.

Numerous polls, self-report surveys, and other studies reveal a significant overall decline in most forms of illegal drug use in America during the 1980s, relative to the 1970s (Goode 1990, 1091; Jensen et al. 1991, 653–55). Nonetheless, during the 1980s, American politicians increasingly made public declarations of a war on drugs. Ronald Reagan made several presidential statements, the first of which occurred in October 1982: "The mood towards drugs is changing in this country and the momentum is with us. We're making no excuses for drugs hard, soft, or otherwise. Drugs are bad and we're going after them" (Reagan, quoted in Wisotsky 1990, 3). In 1989 George Bush made a similar televised declaration. Bush's language, however, was strikingly more militant. Bush invoked numerous signifiers of war, including such terms as "battles," "weapons," "strategy," "winning back neighborhoods block by block," "just cause," and "victory" (Bush, quoted in McGaw 1991, 53–54). Bush and Reagan furthermore depicted drugs and drug users as a dangerous and serious threat to the social and moral fabric of American society, and Bush even made claims that capital punishment is an appropriate punishment for certain drug criminals (See McGaw 1991).

Both Reagan and Bush thoroughly demonized illicit drugs. In fact, as the following quotes illustrate, both politicians construe drugs as the most serious and vile threat to American society:

> Let us not forget who we are. Drug abuse is a
> repudiation of everything that America is. The
> destructiveness and human wreckage mock our
> heritage. . . . Drugs are menacing our society. They're
> threatening our values and undercutting our institutions.

## Social and Historical Context

They're killing our children. (Reagan, quoted in Elwood 1994, 28, 29)

This is the first time since taking the oath of office that I felt an issue was so important, so threatening that it warranted talking with you, the American people. All of us agree that the gravest domestic threat facing our nation today is drugs. . . . Drugs are a real and terribly dangerous threat to our neighborhoods, our friends, and our families. . . . In short, drugs are sapping our strength as a nation. (Bush, quoted in Elwood 1994, 33–34)

According to McGaw (1991), these discursive rhetorical signifiers of the war on drugs became a social reality in the form of laws and law-enforcement practices. Moreover, the war metaphors heightened and broadened public awareness of America's drug problem, increasing its political significance. The moderate public concern of the early 1980s soared to unprecedented levels during the mid- to late 1980s (Jensen et al., 1991,655).

Such pervasive and highly public sentiments have substantial repercussions. Referring back to Matza's ideas on subculture (1969), the war on drugs is precisely the sort of mainstream cultural ethos that encircles, permeates, and thereby offers latent support to phenomena such as straightedge. Indeed, elements of the straightedge subculture reflected the drug war in significant ways throughout the 1980s and into the 1990s.

The potential similarities between the two cultural forms are especially apparent when comparing mainstream drug-war discourse with themes in straightedge music lyrics. In his televised address to the nation, George Bush invoked concepts such as war, victory, and the defense of innocent children: "Neighborhood by neighborhood, block by block, child by child. . . . Victory over drugs is our cause, a just cause, and with your help, we are going to win. . . . It's as innocent looking as candy, but it is turning our cities into battle zones, and it is murdering our children" (Bush, quoted in McGaw 1991, 53, 61).

Very similar images appear in numerous straightedge songs of the early 1990s. One notable example is Earth Crisis's song "Firestorm," which was produced several years after Bush's televised address. The song calls for a straightedge firestorm to purify society of drug lords and drug dealers. The song's opening line is remarkably similar to the opening line in Bush's statement: "Street by street, block by block, taking it all back." Other lines in the song proceed to invoke images of a drug war fought on behalf of innocent victims: "No mercy, no exceptions, a declaration of total war/The innocent's defense, the reason it's waged for" (Earth Crisis 1993a).

Both cultural discourses—the drug-war rhetoric and the straightedge music lyrics—portray drugs, drug users, and drug dealers as threats to the social and moral fabric of American society. Moreover, just as the war on drugs culminated in the rearticulation of domestic police tactics as well as the mobilization of the armed forces in drug interdiction activities (see Kraska 1993, 165–75), themes in straightedge music lyrics often construed straightedgers as subcultural drug warriors. Indeed, around the same time that mainstream drug warriors espoused a "get tough on crime" approach to drug criminals, some elements of the straightedge music genre began to espouse extreme and retributive violence towards all perceived drug enemies.

I do not argue that the mainstream war on drugs somehow created straightedge. Nor do I argue that straightedge could not exist in the absence of America's war on drugs. I do argue, however, that the dynamics of the war on drugs at the very least provided a latently supportive environment for the straightedge phenomenon to flourish and likely impacted many straightedgers' perceptions of the seriousness of America's alleged drug problem. In fact, mainstream culture transmitters disseminated information about the drug war at such a rate that it would have been practically impossible for straightedgers of the late 1980s and early 1990s to not have internalized at least some of the rhetoric.

Throughout the 1980s, media coverage of the drug war increased at an astonishingly quick rate and regularly drew upon the war rhetoric used by politicians (see Elwood 1994, 45; Vila 1993, 34–35). As evidence of this trend, tabulations of entries in the *Reader's Guide to Periodical Literature* suggest a general increase, from 1980 to 1985, in the number of articles published in national magazines dealing with illicit drugs (Goode 1990, 1088). In 1986 alone, national magazines printed a total of 280 articles on the topic of drugs. This marked more than a twofold increase over the previous year and a sixfold increase in less than three years (Goode 1990, 1088; Jensen et al. 1991, 657). The American televised media similarly followed suit. Throughout the 1980s, the major American television networks increasingly broad-cast documentaries, special sitcom episodes, and advertise-ments that strongly adhered to official drug-war rhetoric (Bertram et al. 1996, 113; Elwood 1994; Wisotsky 1990, 5).

Illustrating the effect of the rhetoric, public concern about illicit drugs soared to unprecedented levels by the late 1980s (Jensen et al. 1991, 655). A George Gallup poll, for example, found that the percentage of Americans indicating that drug abuse was "the most important problem facing this country" increased from only 2 percent in 1985 to 38 per-cent in 1989 (Staley 1992, 4). Other polls and surveys gar-ner even more striking results. In August 1986, a US News/CNN poll found that 86 percent of all respondents perceived "fighting the drug problem" as extremely impor-tant (Jensen et al. 1991, 656). Similarly, in 1989, both an in-dependent Media General/Associated Press poll and a Times/CBS poll found that more than 60 percent of all re-spondents ranked drugs as the nation's leading problem compared to the federal deficit, the economy, the environ-ment, and homelessness (Goode 1990, 1088; Staley 1992, 5). In the following year, *Maclean's* magazine found that Americans rated drugs as the second most important na-tional problem (Erickson 1992, 242). Speaking about these apparent increases in public concern, Wisotsky (1990, xvii) claims that, by the late 1980s, the majority of Americans be-lieved that the drug problem was worse than it ever had been.

Further evidence suggests that many American citizens truly internalized drug-war rhetoric and sought to confront the nation's drug problem at a very localized and interpersonal level. During the latter half of the 1980s, the print media contained numerous stories of individual Americans (usually ethnic minority inner-city residents) who sought to mobilize their respective streets, neighborhoods, and schools to engage in "local battles" against drugs (Elwood 1994, 54, 55). Similarly, according to Davis and Lurigio (1996, 16, 42), during the late 1980s, residents of "drug-plagued" areas across the United States initiated numerous block-watch groups, antidrug patrols, marches, and vigils. Citizens also implemented drug-reporting programs and instituted environmental changes in order to deny drug dealers a favorable environment for conducting business. Although such efforts occasionally led to violent confrontations between citizens and alleged drug enemies, officials frequently pledged their support to such private antidrug initiatives (17, 40). Indeed, several of these grassroots initiatives persisted and grew in size and scope, ultimately achieving some level of entrenched organization. Some examples include Mothers Against Gangs in Communities, Let's Clean It Up, and the Direct Truth Antidrug Coalition (Elwood 1994, 55; 60–61).

In light of the apparent fervor with which mainstream cultural agents embraced the drug war, and in light of the sheer number of people exhibiting concern about illicit drugs, it is likely that all straightedge individuals were at least moderately exposed to drug-war rhetoric, and it is likely that at least some of them internalized elements of it. Given the unprecedented increase in both print and televised media coverage of the war on drugs, it seems unlikely that a majority of the youth who comprised the straightedge subculture in the late 1980s could have insulated themselves entirely from the media blitz. These media accounts usually were exaggerated and sensationalized, and they often invoked metaphorical or discursive signifiers of war— the same metaphors and discursive signifiers that later got emulated and transmitted in certain elements of the straightedge music genre.

Consistent with Matza's conception of youth subcultures as "subterranean" traditions (1969), straightedge lyrical references to drugs and drug users, as well as the appearance of hardline in the late 1980s, may at least partially reflect straightedgers' exposure to the mainstream war-on-drugs cultural ethos. Again, I do not argue that the war on drugs creates outright the general straightedge antidrug sentiment. I do argue, however, that its cultural ethos supported and partially refocused an issue that already was important to most straightedge individuals. The ethos provided an environment that encouraged militancy and increasingly coerced new straightedge affiliates into seeing the subculture as a social crusade as well as a personal lifestyle commitment.

It is possible that new straightedge affiliates in the late 1980s derived certain values that were used to partially reconstruct their frame of reference. The war on drugs galvanized around such values and norms as moral purity, judgment, and intolerance. These same values and norms are explicitly manifest in many of the straightedge cultural texts produced during the war-on-drugs era. While the direction of this alleged cultural reinforcement is difficult to prove, the argument that it flows from the mainstream cultural form to the subcultural one may be supported by the fact that the mainstream cultural ethos exercises disproportionate control over powerful culture transmitters such as the mass media.

While the straightedge youth subculture likely reflected and received reinforcement from the mainstream cultural ethos in significant ways, it is important to realize that the subculture also maintains some level of differentiation. Specifically, straightedge differentiates itself by including legal substances into its broader conception of a drug enemy and by advocating illegal violence in combating perceived drug enemies. The war on drugs implies simply that "illegal drugs are bad." They are bad, moreover, because they are detrimental to the moral and social fabric of American society. In contrast, straightedge youth culture, in its strong commitment to moral purity, maintains that even legalized substances can be detrimental to society's moral and social fabric. Thus, while the mainstream war on drugs utilizes legality as a signifier of morality, the straightedge youth culture, by its aversion to legal substances, construes morality as a quality that supersedes legality.

In line with its adherence to legality as a signifier of morality, the mainstream war on drugs openly advocates the use of force and violence only within the boundaries of what the American legal system will allow. The straightedge youth subculture, however, diverges or differentiates itself insofar as it appeals to higher loyalties such as moral purity (see Sykes and Matza 1957) and thereby rationalizes (at least within its cultural texts) the use of aggressive, assaultive, and illegal violence.

# Straightedge Youth

## Summary

Straightedge subcultural boundaries apparently form and get sustained partially in reaction to external cultural forces. At one level, straightedge is a reaction against the nihilism inherent to the punk subculture. At another level, it is a reaction to the mainstream teen culture's celebration of alcohol and drug use as well as promiscuous sexual activity. In addition to reacting to external cultural forces, it is apparent that straightedge cultural boundaries are permeable to those forces. Mainstream drug-war rhetoric, for example, likely infiltrated straightedge cultural boundaries via individuals who were exposed to the war on drugs cultural ethos. Thus, while straightedge individuals claim to maintain their cultural boundaries in reaction to particular mainstream and external cultural forces, these forces paradoxically impact straightedge boundaries internally.

# 6 Straightedge Symbolism

## X-ing Up

**A**s I briefly mentioned earlier in this book, the letter X, and objects superimposed to form the shape of the letter X, have long been symbols of straightedge culture. Often referred to as "X-ing up," some straightedgers draw wide black Xs on the tops of their hands using a felt marker (Irwin 1999, 369). Confirming this, a *48 Hours* documentary portrays straightedge youth X-ing up prior to going to a music gig (Lagatutta 1996). Similarly, *Strife: One Truth Live,* a documentary film of straightedge band Strife on their U.S. tour, includes footage of numerous X-ed up straightedgers queued outside live-music venues (Victory Records 1996). Some embrace the practice of X-ing up to relative extremes, tattooing the symbol on their hands and other parts of their bodies (see, for example, Atkinson 2003). Neil has a tattoo on his forearm depicting a clenched fist with an X on top. Another straightedger, Alan, claimed to have Xs tattooed on his neck. Mail-order catalogues featuring straightedge merchandise, as well as my own observations at straightedge music concerts, further reveal that, in addition to tattooing their bodies, members of the subculture often wear X-shaped symbols on their shirts, jackets, and hats.

Straightedge music sometimes describes the straightedger's relationship to the X as similar to submitting to crucifixion. For example, Bold sings: "Working together, with straight clean souls/NAILED TO THE X" (1988b). Similarly, in a song called "Forged in the Flames," Earth Crisis sings: "Through the veil of shadows, the light of truth is my only guide/A knight unyielding, to the X I'm crucified" (1993b). At a later date, in a song called "Fortress," Earth Crisis further adds: "The X symbolizes my lifetime commitment to live free from their poisons/I've built myself to last" (1995c).

For at least some straightedge youth, the X delineates symbolically the subculture's social network boundaries. The X likely is a means by which straightedge youth identify one another as well as how they demarcate themselves from perceived outsiders. Moreover, according to the music, the X is a means of self-identification insofar as it symbolizes one's commitment and dedication to straightedge philosophy and lifestyles: "X on your hand, now take the oath/To positive youth, to positive growth" (Youth of Today 1997).

Having presented evidence that at least some straightedge individuals display or lay claim to the symbol of the X, readers should be aware that many straightedgers do not. Indeed, a number either do not directly utilize the X, or they do so with some reservations. Twenty-two-year-old Daisy explained: "I hold this [straightedge] philosophy, but I don't see myself . . . wearing Xs on my hand." Allison, also twenty-two, owns some X paraphernalia: "I am wearing a belt right now with an X buckle, and I have sweat-shirts. I have a straightedge sweatshirt, I have an X sister-hood sweatshirt." Allison, however, explained to me that her ownership of these items, rather than being consciously pursued, instead is more a latent manifestation of being part of the straightedge scene: "[T]hey're just kind of some-thing that worked [their] way into the rest of my wardrobe that I don't really think about. It's just on my sweatshirt, y'know?"

## Origins of the X

I asked Ian MacKaye if he had a sense of when and where the connection between the X and straightedge first appeared. He explained that it gained much of its initial momentum in 1980, in his own local hardcore scene in Washington, D.C. According to MacKaye, the X stems from efforts of underage punk rockers to gain admission to shows held in bars and other establishments that prohibited minors:

> In D.C. there was a law that says no minors were
> allowed in a bar; no one under the age of eighteen,
> which was the drinking age at the time. But there was a
> loophole, because also in the District there was a law
> that says if you serve alcohol you have to serve food.
> Then technically there was no such thing as a bar . . . all
> of these places were actually restaurants. They refer to
> them as "popcorn laws" because the food they would
> serve was popcorn. So we were trying to figure out how

we could convince them to let us into these damn gigs, since we had the legal basis for it. . . . The bar owners at the time, they were going with what they saw as the less risky law to break. There was less of a risk to them to deny entrance [by] like basically breaking a discrimination law versus chancing having a kid drinking in their club, which is a liquor law, which is a much more serious thing to deal with. So we had to figure out a way to get into these clubs. So we went down and met with the club and said, "Look, let us in, we will not drink, and we will put these Xs on our hands to clearly demark the people who are under age." We told them, "We don't drink."

I mean, the young kids. We didn't drink, we were playing music, and we were doing [creating] magazines. We were not involved with getting high; we were just working and creating something. And we felt like music was not something that we should be forbidden to absorb, or to see, or to be around just because of our age. So we had been to California in 1980 and . . . went to a club there where they had this X on the hands. So when we came back we said, "Look, let us in, we'll put the Xs on our hands." And the club said, "Yeah." . . . They said, "Let's give it a shot." And we lived up to our end of the bargain, which was that none of us drank. . . . That was where the X came from, it was a total pragmatic thing. . . . The X was really not so much to signify straightedge as it was to signify youth.

According to MacKaye, the X initially was not intended as a symbol of straightedge but as a practical means for young people to gain access to bars and drinking establishments that hosted live punk rock music. The visibility of the X also was functional for the owners of these venues as it helped ensure that they did not inadvertently break any liquor laws by serving alcohol to minors. Thus, as MacKaye explains, the X began more as a symbol of youthfulness than as a symbol of straightedge.

Despite the pragmatics that surround the earliest iteration of the X, MacKaye points out that it gradually assumed an added level of meaning: "I turned eighteen in 1980. I was even old enough to drink. All of us punk rockers, even if we were twenty-five, were putting Xs on our hands to sort of show solidarity to the concept that there was a certain segment, a large segment, of the audience that was just not going to drink." Thus, very early on, during the genesis of the subculture, the X became a basis for solidarity and a symbol of unity among straightedge punk rockers. Just as MacKaye and his friends first encountered the X in California, and then brought the idea home with them to Washington, D.C., it was probably similarly transmitted from one punk scene to another across the United States, Canada, and other Western countries. Transmission of early straightedge symbolism likely occurred through informal social network ties, touring bands, as well as through fanzines and music recordings, which can be distributed widely in a relatively short period of time.

Porcell, former guitar player for Youth of Today, confirms the role that music and touring played in the rapid transmission of straightedge symbolism:

## Straightedge Youth

We [Youth of Today] came out and we were very vocal, we were very straightedge, and we put these big black Xs on our hands. This was before there was a whole straightedge movement; there was a few straightedge bands. . . . Our single came out, and I remember playing CBGB's and thinking, "Oh my God, am I going to put this X on my hand, or am I gonna get beat up by fifteen skinheads if I do?" Then "Break Down the Walls" [an album] came out, and we did a whole tour. And then we came back to New York. I couldn't believe it. We were playing the same CBGB that, less than a year before, I was scared to put the X on my hand. We show up and play, and there's, like, tons of straightedge kids with Xs on their hands, and singing along to "Thinking Straight." And I remember thinking, this is amazing. I never thought that it was actually going to take off into a whole sort of thing where Youth of Today could go on tour around the country, and every single show that we play, there's a contingent of the hardcore scene with Xs on their hands, and the whole straightedge look I guess, and they're singing along, and they know every word. I can't really explain it myself, but it was a real phenomenon.

## Iterations of the X

Since the early 1980s, the X has been continually reconstructed or reiterated by straightedge individuals. These iterations often take the form of a standard-looking, although usually bold letter X surrounded by words or slogans intended to communicate a particular type of straightedge stance. Other times, iterations comprise common objects superimposed in the image of an X. Some notable examples found on the covers of straightedge fanzines and music recordings include crossed judge's gavels (Judge 1989b), crossed baseball bats (Diehard 1989), crossed shovels (Six Feet Deep 1994), and crossed hockey sticks. The latter example is associated with a band called Slapshot. Occasionally, on gig posters and album covers, the crossed hockey sticks get superimposed against or beside an image of a hockey goalie's shattered mask.

Images such as these, combined with band names, for some observers may merge together into a system of meaning. Crossed baseball bats in conjunction with the name Diehard, for example, may communicate a stance of defending and holding one's ground (Diehard 1989). The crossed bats also may indicate impending confrontation as well as a gate through which transgressors must pass. While I only can speculate, it is plausible that these implied meanings reflect something of the band members' personal life experiences. Indeed, in a fanzine interview, Dwid, a former member of Diehard, reflects upon some past experiences that appear to parallel the Diehard theme:

> People would put us down, me and my friends. . . .
> They'd try to insult us, and some people would take it in
> stride. But I'm not the kind of person to do that and I'd
> get into fights. . . . When I would retaliate against the
> jock guys, or the mainstream people . . . I'd be the one
> to get all the punishment. After a few instances of

defending my friends' names, and my own name, I got
expelled. (Dwid, cited in *We Shall Fight in the Streets*
1995)

For Dwid, fighting and defending himself against antagonists
became, at least for a while, a regular facet of his lifestyle.
The implied militancy of the Diehard name and logo, therefore, may be a reflection of Dwid's life experiences at the
time.

Jack (also known as "Choke") is the lead singer of Slapshot, and I asked him about the origin of the band's name as
well as its associated symbols. Jack explained that the name
stemmed originally from his love of hockey as well as his
appreciation of the popular film *Slapshot*: "I've always been
a hockey fan. . . . we were thinking, like, how about ice
hockey terms? Power play, cross checking, and then it was
like, hey, how about "slapshot"? We love the movie! It [the
name and the symbols] all went together." Thus, in the case
of Slapshot, the name simply made sense. It reflected something of the band members' personal tastes; they perceived
it as humorous in its connection with a popular film, and it
sounded appropriately straightedge in its implied militancy.
The band's associated images of crossed hockey sticks and
smashed goalie masks are simply a logical outgrowth of the
hockey theme articulated within a distinctly straightedge
context.

Mike, the lead singer of the now-disbanded Judge, similarly explains his own perceptions of how the band's name
and associated symbols originated. In an interview with
Beth Lahickey (1997, 78–79, 87), Mike explains that Judge

## Straightedge Symbolism

at least partially emerged in response to the negative reactions that straightedge garnered among elements of the hardcore music scene during the late 1980s:

> The ideas that I had at that point were kind of negative because I was a little pissed off the way Youth of Today was treated. It was kind of stupid of me, I guess. I was mad at these people who were saying that we were these elitist, Nazi-type straightedge guys. Instead of trying to do something to prove that they were wrong and that we weren't like that, I guess we went the full other circle and decided to give them a little bit of what they thought we were about. . . . They want something elitist, and they want something militant, then what could be more elitist and militant than calling the band "Judge"?

Mike claims to have consciously contrived the symbols and associated meanings surrounding Judge in reaction to hostility from other elements of the hardcore scene.

While at least some straightedge symbolism is subjectively constructed, according to the perceptions and life experiences of its creators, evidence suggests that constructions and reiterations can be coercive upon those who receive or apprehend them. Speaking about his observations of violence at music gigs, Mike alludes to the coercive effects of the meanings and images surrounding Judge: "People had these perception[s] of what I was about and what Judge was about. In some cases they might have been a little bit right, but they just expected something different than

Judge or what Judge was about. When we got there, there was a whole lot of fights everywhere. . . . There was so much violence at all the shows" (quoted in Lahickey 1997, 79).

During my interview with Porcell (another former member of Judge), he confirms Mike's observations, suggesting that the symbolism of the band might have unintentionally fostered violent intolerance within audiences:

> The last tour we ever went on in America, it was completely disheartening, because there was just so many fights at every show. Y'know, a kid with an X on his hand would come up to me after the show and start telling me how he just beat the crap out of some guy that had a beer in his hand . . . as if he was impressing me or something. And I tell you, at the end of the tour, me and the singer, I remember we even had a little meeting about it. We were just like, we're gonna break up. . . . It's such a horrible thing to know that you could have impacted a person in such a negative way. . . . Even if people are misunderstanding the message, it's still not worth it.

Porcell's and Mike's words suggest that, while straightedge culture is subjectively and socially constructed, it may have an objective impact upon future members of the subculture. Artifacts like symbols, lyrics, and band names may coalesce into a system of reified and objectified meaning. Thus, while Judge emerged as a subjectively constructed reaction to criticism and perceived hostility, the implied mili-

tancy of the Judge concept has become over time an unin-
tended and partial frame of reference that may define, at
least for some individuals, what straightedge is all about. It
acts as a coercive concept insofar as it may structure and
constrain how people form for themselves a straightedge
identity, as well as how they interact with others.

## The X and Identity Categorization

According to Fiske's interpretation of Levi-Strauss (1990,
116–17), people make sense of the world through the construction of binary oppositions. Fiske explains:

> A binary opposition is a system of two related categories
> that, in its purest form, comprises the universe. In the
> perfect binary opposition, everything is either in
> category A or category B, and by imposing such
> categories upon the world we are starting to make sense
> of it. So category A cannot exist on its own, as an
> essential category, but only in a structured relationship
> with category B: category A makes sense because it is
> not category B. Without category B there could be no
> boundary to category A and thus no category A. (1990,
> 116)

Fiske (119–20) goes on to explain that the vital importance of categories in society has universally produced a series of boundary rituals, which are designed to ease the
transition from one category to another. A marriage cere-

mony, for example, might be seen as a boundary ritual signifying the transition between single and married life.

Based on Fiske's interpretation of Levi-Strauss, I argue that the act of claiming the X, and the X in and of itself (at least within a straightedge context), represents something of a boundary ritual. The X demarcates straightedge boundaries, and it identifies those who have made a personal transition into a straightedge identity. Indeed, it also distinguishes the wearer from perceived outsiders, and it signifies various levels of meaning. In the first instance, it embodies something of a public claim about the wearer's identity. The X, however, not only displays to others the message "I am straightedge," but it is also an act of self-affirmation. To the prospective straightedger, the act of displaying or claiming the X may constitute an ontological affirmation of the self. It signifies to the wearer that he or she has in fact crossed a boundary and facilitates the person's own self-categorization.

Having made this argument about "claiming the X" as a boundary ritual, I must also emphasize that not all straightedge individuals require the X as signification of their straightedge identity. Indeed, as I mentioned earlier, many straightedge individuals do not wear the X, and to many of them its presence in their lives is simply a latent manifestation of being around straightedge culture. Sociologists of religion often address the issue of internal-versus-external religious affiliation. External affiliation describes those people who place a great importance on external symbols and observable practices of religious life, regarding them as signifiers of their inner faith. Internal affiliation, in contrast, describes those people who instead emphasize the internal-ization of religious beliefs and values, and place compara-tively less importance on observable symbols and rituals (Kirkpatrick 1993). In the same way, it is plausible that some straightedge individuals may be more prone to emphasizing either an external or internal affiliation. Thus, rather than being a face-value measure of one's "straightedgeness," it is possible that the X simply is more likely to be utilized by ex-ternally affiliated straightedge individuals when compared to those who are more internally affiliated. In cases where the X does get claimed and displayed, it can become a pow-erful and effective transmitter of straightedge ideology.

## The X and the Transmission Ideology

Ideologies are systems of belief that latently reflect the con-text of their production, as well as manifestly reflect the subjectivity of the producers (Goode 1992). Once con-structed, ideologies can be internalized and reconstructed by other individuals, wherein the ideology organizes the in-dividual's attitudes into a coherent pattern (Fiske 1990, 165). Once they are internalized, ideologies are highly co-ercive insofar as they mobilize people into action and artic-ulate and integrate their life experiences into a framework of meaning that exists outside the realm of the individual's own subjectivity.

Symbols, such as the straightedge X, are a central com-ponent of ideology. In a discussion of the relationship be-tween symbols and ideology, John Fiske (1990, 171) explains that symbols give concrete form to ideology, and in doing so, they both endorse it and make it public. Furthermore, in using symbols "we maintain and give life to ideology, but we are also formed by that ideology, and by our response to ideological signs." Thus, according to Fiske, the use of things such as cultural signs and symbols translates into a situation where ideology becomes a form of practice: "In participating in the signifying practices of my culture I am the means by which ideology maintains itself. The meanings I find in a sign derive from the ideology within which the sign and I exist: by finding these meanings I define myself in relation to the ideology and in relation to my society" (172).

Based on Fiske's ideas, the X can be viewed as a powerful transmitter of straightedge ideology as well as a marker of expanding straightedge subcultural boundaries. In claiming the X, the individual communicates the existence of straightedge and makes a public claim that "straightedge is here, now, in this time and space." Some people, when encountering the X, may simply look through it. Indeed, for many people, perhaps it holds no resonance, and consequently they feel no need to engage the symbol in any way whatsoever. For example, perhaps you, the reader, have encountered a straightedge individual. Perhaps you have actually observed straightedge displays of the X, and perhaps you looked right past the symbolism because it simply holds no meaning for you. Conversely, you may have encountered the X in circumstances where you feel compelled to engage it. Suppose, for example, that you have a teenage child, and that child suddenly begins to draw a black X on his or her hand every single morning. You ask your child why she does this, and she explains to you that she does it because she is straightedge. In that instant, something of straightedge ideology gets transmitted as if it were an electrical impulse crossing a synaptic gap. From that moment on, you likely will engage the X at some level of meaning each time you encounter it.

Cultural transmissions, in crossing the gap from one subjective individual to another, lose traces and components of their point of origin. By definition, one person can not fully know the subjectivity of another. Thus, while two people displaying the X may encounter one another, and while both people understand the symbol within the context of the straightedge cultural ethos, each person's claim to the X will be at least slightly different. Hence, we see variations and iterations of the X, each with its own implied or suggested meanings.

## Conclusion

Straightedgers commonly identify themselves as well as their cultural spaces and artifacts with an X or objects crossed to resemble an X. Straightedge ideology gets transmitted through X symbolism, iterations of which denote shifts or variations in the ideology. Indeed, particular straightedge individuals, as well as localized straightedge networks, may articulate novel variations of the X as a means of communicating a subjective or regional stance on the meaning of straightedge.

While many straightedge individuals actively and consciously display X symbolism, many others do not. Some maintain no identification with it, while for others the X infiltrates daily life only as a latent consequence of being immersed in straightedge culture. It is plausible that people who do and do not place great importance on X symbolism can be distinguished respectively by external and internal affiliation with straightedge ideals. For externally affiliated individuals, claiming the X likely embodies a boundary ritual symbolizing the individual's transition into a new identity.

Regardless of individual or collective associations with X symbolism, the X encodes and concretizes a subjective straightedge stance that ultimately coerces others who later apprehend that symbol. Recall Mike's explanation that the band Judge, as well as its trademark X (consisting of crossed judge's gavels), was consciously contrived as a reaction to hostility and prejudice directed towards straightedgers in the New York area during the late 1980s. Mike and other band members explained that the militant themes and meanings surrounding Judge served to incite hostility and even violence within the music scene. While the name and symbols associated with Judge had their genesis in the subjective associations of the band's members, they came to embody certain themes and meanings that ultimately coerced and constrained at least some straightedgers, who later affiliated themselves with both the band and its symbolism. Thus, iterations of the X are based upon past subjective expressive human activity. These iterations take on an objective existence and ultimately may coerce future straightedgers who apprehend the symbol and its meanings.

## Straightedge Symbolism

Future researchers may benefit by revisiting the signs and symbols used by contemporary youth subcultures. In particular, analysis of those signs and symbols may prove fruitful in studies of subcultural identity. More specifically, not only could researchers further explore the ways in which symbols not only unify and identify subcultures in collective ways, but they could also explore the manner in which symbols shape and maintain subcultural identities at an individual level.

# 7 Toward a Theory of Subcultural Change and Schism

## Conceptualizing Subcultural Schism

**S**ince the early 1980s, it is clear that straightedge has endured at least several noteworthy boundary transitions, which may best be described as schisms. Schism is the division of a social group into two or more relatively distinct and opposed factions (Bainbridge 1978, 1991; Barbu 1996; Gustafson 1978; Hood-Brown et al. 1991; Stark and Bainbridge 1985, 1987; Starke and Dyck 1996). Schism has long been evident, although sometimes overlooked, in other youth subcultures. Researchers conclude, for example, that the American and Canadian skinhead subcultures fragmented during the 1980s and 1990s into a number of ideologically distinct factions, including racist skinheads, antiracist skinheads, communist skinheads, and nonpolitical skinheads (Coplon 1988; Moore 1993; Wood 1999b; Young and Craig 1997; Zellner 1995). Similarly, researchers of the British skinhead subculture suggest that it evolved from the hard-mod subculture, and that the hard mods themselves emerged at least partially as a schismatic faction of the larger mod subculture (see Brake 1993; Cohen 1972; Hamm 1993; Kinsella 1994; Moore 1993).

## Subcultural Change and Schism

In the straightedge case, we see evidence of schism in at least several obvious respects. The subculture itself arguably emerged as a schismatic faction of the early 1980s punk subculture, galvanizing around a militant opposition to punk's celebrations of alcohol, drugs, and casual sex. During the mid—to late 1980s, straightedge scenes across the United States apparently began to seek some level of distance and separation from the broader punk phenomenon. Furthermore, into the late 1980s and early 1990s, at least two relatively distinct factions emerged: a militant hardline faction and the Krishna Conscious variant. Moreover, into the mid—and late 1990s, it seems that at least a small minority of straightedge affiliates were forging ideological links to the allegedly satanic organization, The Process Church of Final Judgment. Denoting a rift in the subcultural frame of reference, each faction galvanizes or relates in some way to the straightedge concept, yet articulates a different meaning of the subculture and elaborates a different conception of what being a member is all about. These factions and rifts represent evolving cultural configurations. They emerge as new constellations of straightedge culture.

### Social-Psychological Bases of Subcultural Schism

Although schism is most clearly evident in rifts at the level of the subculture's frame of reference, the straightedge case suggests that schism has its roots in microcosmic social-psychological dynamics. New recruits to an already-established subculture may affiliate themselves with the group because they are attracted to its subcultural frame of reference. The potential straightedger, for example, may be attracted by the prospect of what it means to be straightedge as well as what the subculture is all about. The individual may have grown up in, and still reside in, an environment where alcohol and drugs are construed as wrong and immoral. Thus, upon initial contact with straightedge culture, the recruit already might be grappling with a fear or discontent about alcohol and drugs. In turn, the straightedge frame of reference articulates the potential recruit's discontent, delineating its source, construing it as a threat, and proscribing an appropriate set of norms, values, and beliefs for overcoming it. As long as the subcultural frame of reference properly articulates the individual's discontent, he or she will remain affiliated with the subculture. When and if the individual continues to feel discontented, however, he or she may cease to identify with the subculture. Thus, subcultural schism likely finds its earliest points of genesis in situations where a member continues to feel discontented or to perceive a threat, but the subcultural frame of reference fails to provide a sufficient level of articulation and resolution. In these instances, that individual may seek to modify the subculture's frame of reference such that it does provide sufficient articulation and resolution.

The case of the Krishna Conscious offshoot is an excellent example of this process. Indeed, speaking with straightedgers who later became Krishna Conscious devotees, it is clear that many of these individuals distanced themselves from straightedge because its ideals came to resonate differently with them over time. As an example of this, Porcell explained to me that, prior to becoming Krishna Conscious, he was "getting introspective about why [he] was straightedge in the first place." Referring to the late 1980s New York straightedge scene, he said that he felt incredibly jaded with it in general:

> All the straightedge kids grew up, and they started going to college, and they grew their hair out, and then straightedge became, like, an uncool thing. . . . And, you know, then you see, like, there is these other straightedge kids, and they're assholes, and they're beating people up. And there's other people that drink and they seem pretty cool. So, what actually is the goal? Is the goal to become straightedge, or is the goal to become a better person? So, I was starting to realize that, just drinking, it wasn't the end, it wasn't the all in all. And I just thought that [straightedge] was a good foundation for something else.

Porcell further explains that straightedge did not properly facilitate a lifestyle based on his ideals, and that Krishna Consciousness helped him to attain such a lifestyle: "I was always idealistic, but I didn't always live perfectly up to my ideals. . . . And I am in a band singing, 'Make a change, make a change, make a change,' and I am finding it difficult to even make a change in myself. And that's when I realized, it's not enough to scream 'Make a change.' You have to learn how to do that."

Ray Cappo (lead singer for Youth of Today) also communicates a sense of being deeply frustrated with the straightedge scene prior to converting to Krishna Consciousness:

"The straightedge scene got so big, but it seemed to be more like a fashion statement rather than anyone seriously trying to improve themselves. . . . I thought the whole scene was getting misguided. I don't know if I misguided it, or if people in general misguided it, but they were getting into straight-edge for the wrong reasons. It wasn't for self-purification, it was more for ego trips and fashion" (Ray Cappo, quoted in Lahickey 1997, 30–31).

After becoming Krishna Conscious, both Porcell and Cappo expressed a sense of satisfaction with the transition. Ray in particular was able to reconcile his discontent with the straightedge music scene as well as his role as a musician within that scene:

> The Krishna philosophy isn't to renounce anything
> falsely, but if you're good at something, you should use it
> in the service of Krishna, not just neglect it. So I tried to
> renounce music, but it's part of my nature to do music,
> to write music. So you use the same music, but you do it
> spiritually. That's what I think Shelter is. . . . It's the same
> exact thing, but with more of a spiritual twist. At the
> same time, we follow certain spiritual principles; we're
> celibate, we're vegetarians, we're straight. (Ray Cappo,
> quoted in Lahickey 1997, 31, 33)

Also asserting some level of discontent with his involvement in the scene, Porcell made it very clear to me that his straightedge identity did not fully allow him to satisfy his ideals and principles. However, after becoming Krishna

## Subcultural Change and Schism

Conscious, he lived on a farm where his lifestyle became much more satisfying:

> It was such a different lifestyle. Such a higher lifestyle than I was used to living; y'know, waking up at noon and watching TV and stuff like that. It was such a boost, and plus I felt really good about myself because now I am really living up to what I believe. I was against pollution, I was against the whole way that Americans live their life, it's just so horrible. . . . It's just like people have no concept of working with the earth and not against the earth. It was great. We were growing all our own food there, we had cows, we were taking care of all kinds of animals. And I really felt like, now I am living a lifestyle that's conducive with everything I think and believe.

Here, in addition to expressing a heightened sense of satisfaction, Porcell suggests that Krishna Consciousness enabled him to live a lifestyle more congruent with the principles that he had held all along.

Thus, as explained by Porcell and Cappo, the transition from one subcultural identity to another emerges from a process of identity confrontation. The existing frame of reference no longer satisfactorily articulates the individual's sense of self and identity. Thus, the shift from one cultural affiliation into another is a practical attempt to relieve a sense of dissonance about one's own identity as well as a means of rearticulating feelings of discontent that led to the initial subcultural affiliation. Indeed, Porcell explains that his feeling of discontent with society and with his own lifestyle initially led to him to affiliate with straightedge. However, it was insufficient in bringing about the changes that he sought, and so he encountered the Krishna Consciousness movement as an alternate avenue of realizing his goals and articulating his discontent and perceptions of the social world.

In sum, it is plausible that schism, at the most basic level, begins when the subcultural frame of reference no longer articulates the individual's sense of discontent. Consequently, the discontented person may seek to modify the subculture frame of reference, or he or she may seek an alternate frame of reference that is more satisfactory.

## Ideological Induction and Alternate Frames of Reference

When speaking with Porcell about his conversion to Krishna Consciousness, he mentioned that he encountered it near the end of a thorough spiritual and religious search. He explained that he felt spirituality was lacking in his life, yet all bodies of spiritual and religious thought seemed to him inadequate until he encountered Krishna Consciousness. During our conversation, I found myself wondering what was so different about Krishna Consciousness and why Porcell chose it over any other form of religion or spirituality. He explained that living a Krishna-Conscious lifestyle not only made sense but also was a relatively easy transition to endure as a result of already having lived a straightedge lifestyle for so many years. In fact, according to Porcell, the transition was facilitated by the fact that straightedge and

## Subcultural Change and Schism

Krishna-Conscious lifestyles are similar in a number of fundamental respects:

> To me it was just like a natural progression of
> straightedge. . . . To me, it, like, clicked, you know what
> I mean? So, in that sense it wasn't such a big progression
> because all the basic tenets of Krishna Consciousness I
> was already following. . . . To me it's sort of like the
> culmination of what straightedge really should be. What
> is the purpose of straightedge? The purpose of
> straightedge is not to put something in your head that's
> going to screw you up and make you think unclearly.
> Okay, once you've cleared your head, now what? Now
> what are you gonna think about? It's not an all in all, it's
> just a means to an end.

For Porcell, Krishna Consciousness seemed like a natural progression because it validated a lifestyle he had been living all along. In other words, he was predisposed to convert to Krishna Consciousness as a result of his prior internalization of straightedge ideals and lifestyle tenets.

The basic Krishna-Conscious lifestyle tenets share remarkable similarities with straightedge. According to A. C. Bhaktivedanta Swami Prabhupada, the founder of the International Society for Krishna Consciousness (ISKCON), all Krishna devotees are called to abide by four regulatory lifestyle principles. These include: (1) no eating of meat, fish, or eggs; (2) no gambling; (3) no sex other than for procreation within marriage; and (4) no intoxication, including recreational drugs, alcohol, tobacco, tea, and coffee. According to official movement teachings, not living in accordance with these regulative principles "disrupts our physical, mental, and spiritual well being and increases anxiety and conflict in society." Living in accordance with the four regulatory principles allegedly enables individuals to control "the insatiable urges of the mind and senses" (Prabhupada 1993, 113) and thereby achieve spiritual enlightenment (3). Thus, with the exception of prohibitions against gambling, the Krishna Consciousness movement's regulatory principles strongly resemble the fundamental straightedge lifestyle tenets. Implying the significance of these similarities, Porcell further explains that conversion to Krishna Consciousness happens often among the straightedge scene: "I know a lot of kids that got into it seriously. I know a lot of devotees who were straightedge kids. I am not just saying this, but it seems that the people from back in the whole youth-crew days who managed to stay straightedge, I'd say most of them are devotees."

Other research strongly suggests that ideological similarities, such as those evidenced between straightedge and Krishna Consciousness, may predispose straightedge individuals (relative to nonstraightedge individuals) to convert to Krishna Consciousness. On the topic of conversion experiences, researchers suggest that conversion stems not primarily from movement structure or recruitment activities (see Rochford 1983, 298; 1982, 408; Snow et al. 1980, 787; Snow and Machalek 1984, 182) but rather from what the Krishna Consciousness movement has to offer ideologically (Wallis and Bruce 1982, 104). For example, Rochford discovers that a substantial number of Hare Krishna devotees

"emphasize the linkage between their premovement cognitive orientations and the movement's ideology and way of
life" (1985, 68). In particular, he finds that "82 percent of the
devotees either were vegetarians or had at least attempted
to regulate their consumption of meat before joining
ISKCON. . . . [O]thers also found the movement's stance
against drugs and other intoxicants appealing" (72).

Kent (1993, 2001) similarly finds evidence that some
devotees' preconversion orientations were compatible with
the ideals of the Krishna Consciousness movement. During
an interview, a former political activist reports to Kent: "A
strong part of the attraction of devotees for me was their
sheer defiant otherwordliness. Because . . . my ideology
basically was just [that] the world as it is is just in such bad
shape that it's not worth saving" (quoted in Kent 1993, 48).
In several studies of American former political activists'
conversion to new religious movements during the early
1970s, Kent (1988, 1993, 2001) provides groundwork for a
more elaborate conception of ideological predisposition.
According to Kent, the power redistribution movement of
the late 1960s and the new religious movements of the early
1970s "shared the same basic goals" (1988, 114). Thus,
claiming that many former political activists adopted the
means and norms of new religious movements as an alternate mode of achieving social movement goals, Kent con-
cludes: "Religious ideology . . . provided the cognitive
avenues by which many former activists reduced the dissonance caused by their commitment to an apparently failed
social movement" (1988, 114). In another study, he further
implies that new religious movements attracted former ac-

tivists by incorporating the "radical rhetorics of opposition" characteristic of the politically oriented social movements of the 1960s (1993, 45–46).

Kent's assertion about the similarity of social and new religious movement goals, coupled with his allusion to continuities between secular and religious movement discourses, implies that former 1960s political activists ideologically were susceptible to joining new religious movements of the 1970s. Indeed, Kent construes former activists' conversions to new religious movements as "shifts of allegiance" (1988, 114). He implies thereby at least some level of compatibility between converts' pre—and postconversion ideology. Stated simply, some converts' preconversion ideals facilitated their transition into new religious movements.

Consistent with other researchers' findings, the preconversion ideals of straightedge converts largely were Krishna-Conscious compatible. Having said this, however, I do not mean to imply that all or even most straightedgers will seek to become Krishna Conscious. Instead, what I do mean is that the ideological similarities between the two cultural forms increase the probability of conversion.

**Social Network Cliques**

Thus far I argue that schism and change in a subculture stems initially from the individual's sense of unarticulated or persisting discontent. The discontent of one individual, however, can not sustain the emergence of an entire subcultural faction. Borrowing concepts from the sociology of religion as well as of social networks, it is possible to explain how microcosmic, individual-level sentiments evolve into the emergence of a full-blown subculture faction.

In elaborating their general theory of religion, Stark and Bainbridge claim:

> All [religious] organizations [comprise] social networks, which consist of the interpersonal relationships among members of the organization. . . . Groups differ in the degree to which their members are attached to one another. . . . Individuals within a group may differ not only in their number of attachments to others, but in the distribution of their ties to others. . . . If we map the complete set of attachments within a group, we may find cleavages—lines of weak attachment between cliques (subnetworks that are internally strongly connected)—persons being attached mainly to members of the same clique. (1985, 101)

Adopting the Stark and Bainbridge description of religious group cleavage, I propose that, through sustained interaction, clusters of similarly subculturally affiliated, yet discontented, individuals may form intrasubcultural cliques. Cliques provide early momentum to the emergent subcultural schism. Bainbridge also implies the schismatic quality of network cliques in his comprehensive study of the Process Church of Final Judgment. In particular, detailing the evolution of the Process Church from the ranks of a psychotherapy group, Bainbridge claims that the cult emerged through a process of "social implosion" (1978, 51).

According to Bainbridge, "In a social implosion, part of an extended social network collapses as social ties within it strengthen and, reciprocally, those to persons outside it weaken. [Social implosion] is a step by step process. . . . [that] may be set off by more than one kind of circumstance" (51–52). Thus, through sustained interaction, clusters of subculturally affiliated yet discontented individuals may form a subculture clique. Given the right circumstances and mitigating factors, in a process of social implosion, the clique members will strengthen their ties with one another while concurrently dissolving attachments to subcultural members affiliated outside the clique boundaries. Consequently, the clique becomes relatively free to construct a modified version of the original subcultural frame of reference.

Theorizing about the emergence, evolution, and schism of new religious groups, Bainbridge proposes, "Frequently a group will add and subtract culture in order to differentiate itself from another group that owns the original culture" (1997, 260). Past studies imply that Bainbridge's ideas apply also to contemporary youth subcultures. Racist and nonracist factions of the American skinhead subculture, for example, stylistically remained similar, yet each faction adopted different subcultural symbols. Racist skinheads marked their bodies, clothes, magazines, and subcultural spaces with distinctly Nazi symbols such as the swastika and the death's head (Hamm 1993). Nonracist skinheads, however, adopted symbols that communicate themes of racial harmony. A common example among nonracist skinheads is a nylon patch depicting white and dark hands clasped in greeting (Wood 1999b). In the same way, it is apparent that certain straightedge franchises and network cliques selectively retain, discard, or reconstruct elements of the original culture in order to communicate a subjective and novel stance on the meaning of straightedge.

Once established, the schismatic clique's alternate subcultural frame of reference (along with its demarcating social and material phenomena) may entice new recruits. Moreover, the schismatic subcultural frame of reference may be transmitted to members of distant networks who apprehend it as a means of alleviating unresolved discontent. Thus, over time, with the accumulation of new recruits and the co-optation of formerly rival adherents, the original clique may evolve into a relatively large faction replete with a distinct frame of reference and comprising possibly numerous franchises. At this point, the subcultural schism is entrenched.

## Culture Engines

According to Bainbridge, "Occasionally in human society a special configuration of social relationships, motives, native talent, and ideas can generate culture at an extremely rapid rate" (1997, 251). Bainbridge refers to such configurations as "culture engines" (1997, 251). The reader may recall my earlier discussion of the apparent timeliness of straightedge. In particular, Ian MacKaye and others explain that the initial idea of straightedge tapped into a latent sentiment present in the American punk scene. MacKaye's song "Straight Edge" was something of a spark that ignited a rapid cultural growth. In other words, MacKaye's ideas were fuel for a straightedge culture engine. Furthermore, over the subculture's history it is apparent that other ideologues have been influential in generating novel iterations of straightedge culture.

Subcultures do not necessarily appear or evolve in a slow and incremental manner. On the contrary, the initial subcultural configuration may appear rapidly within the space of months or a few years. The punk case supports this assertion. While various underlying conditions and influential factors primed or facilitated the emergence of punk, it is a phenomenon that appeared in its explicitly self-conscious form within the space of a year. Similarly, while numerous underlying social factors primed the emergence of straightedge, the phenomenon appeared very quickly during the early 1980s. Indeed, the same pattern characterizes the emergence of distinctly racist and antiracist skinhead subcultural factions in America during the mid—to late 1980s. These cases illustrate the importance of culture engines in mobilizing latent sentiments and thereby generating new forms of culture at a relatively rapid rate.

Not all discontented subculture network cliques will successfully induce a schism. The clique must generate alternate norms, values, and beliefs and successfully recruit or co-opt new members at a rate sufficiently quick enough to resist a twofold threat that all schismatic factions must surmount. Like the entrenched subculture, the schismatic faction maintains an ongoing resistance to mainstream acculturation. More immediately, it must combat the encroachment of the original subculture and possibly other competing schismatic subcultural factions. This latter struggle may involve battles for domination of territorial spaces, pools of potential recruits, or the frame of reference in general. Only those rare factions that successfully become culture engines can surmount this twofold threat.

Discontent is a necessary yet rarely sufficient condition for a subcultural clique to become a culture engine. In order for the clique to evolve into a successful culture engine, it must apprehend a guiding ideology that articulates its members' feelings of discontent. Suitable articulating ideologies are contingent upon numerous intersecting and changing psychological, social, cultural, and historical trajectories. Schism, therefore, is difficult to predict. This aside, several contemporary subcultures provide insight into at least a few facilitators of schism.

In some instances, articulating alternate ideologies stem from external organizations and ideologues that seek to engineer a subcultural schism for the purposes of co-opting at least one of the schismatic factions. The co-optation of American skinheads by the White Aryan Resistance (WAR) is a good example of this possibility. Researchers claim that the American skinhead subculture generally did not galvanize around racism during the early 1980s (Coplon 1988; Wood 1999b). During the middle and later 1980s, however (following the British National Front's successful co-optation of skinheads in the United Kingdom), leaders of the American-based WAR actively sought out skinheads for the purposes of revitalizing the dwindling ranks of the racist right in America. Thus, noting WAR's vigorous skinhead recruitment and indoctrination campaign, researchers identify its ideals as a primary facilitator of the dramatic increase in skinhead racism and active racist skinhead subculture networks during the late 1980s (Hamm 1993).

The straightedge case suggests that budding schismatic subcultural factions may also derive a necessary alternate articulating ideology from the dominant or parent culture. There exists evidence of this in the apparent links between straightedge discourses and those that characterize the American "war on drugs." Indeed, one could argue that the mainstream American war on drugs ideals provided early straightedge punks a requisite alternate ideology to form a schismatic culture engine, and thereby transcend a commonly perceived threat posed by the nihilism and liberalism of punk culture as well as the general moral decay of mainstream teen culture.

## Summary

The straightedge case yields important implications for the conceptualization of subculture schism. Like many other contemporary youth subcultures, including the British mod subculture of the 1960s and the American skinhead subculture of the 1980s, straightedge seems to have bifurcated, possibly several times, into competing subcultural factions.

At one level, such examples of schism indicate a rift in the subculture's frame of reference. They represent a new corpus of overarching norms, values, and beliefs, in relation to which current and future members can form and articulate a subcultural identity. It is important to reiterate that these broad rifts in the boundaries of a subculture are rooted in microcosmic processes of social interaction. Indeed, schisms find their genesis in the discontent of individual subculture members, who may feel that the existing frame of reference insufficiently articulates their perceptions and experiences. Given the right combination of conditions, these individuals might espouse new ideas that mobilize latent sentiments shared by a critical mass of subculture members. This critical mass may then become—again, if conditions are right—a culture engine, generating and expanding new cultural forms with astonishing momentum.

We cannot properly understand any kind of historical change in the nature or composition of a subculture by examining the change solely at a microcosmic or a macrocosmic level. The macrocosmic structures of the subculture and the microcosmic social interactions and identity processes that occur within the constraints of those structures are inextricably linked. Thus, any examination of historical change in a subculture must adopt a two-tiered approach, focusing particularly on the ways in which the macro and the micro each impact the development of the other through a dialectical relationship of mutual coercion.

# 8 Conclusion

## The Complexity and Diversity of Straightedge

Subcultures are curious entities. Especially curious is the fact that we often talk about them as though they are singular and homogeneous objects; as literal things with neat and easily identifiable boundaries, and with a substance that is internally consistent, much like a drinking glass encapsulating a quantity of homogenized milk. Indeed, we tend to paint subcultures with broad brushstrokes, making general claims about the norms, values, and beliefs of the group: "skinheads are racist," "punks are violent," "rrriot grrrls are feminist," and of course, "straightedgers hate drugs." Such general descriptions have some basis in reality, but they tragically oversimplify the many nuanced complexities that characterize contemporary subcultures. Moreover, by essentializing subcultures in such general terms, we run the risk of painting with equally broad brushstrokes the individuals who create, comprise, and sustain subcultures.

Clearly, the straightedge subculture is anything but a monolithic and homogeneous entity. On the contrary, it is characterized by a rich and complex history, with members who are diverse and often uniquely different in their percep-

**148**

tions and understandings of the straightedge concept. Thus, in concluding this book, I think it is appropriate to summarize and highlight aspects of straightedge complexity and diversity, characteristics with important implications for the future conceptualization of subculture.

## The Diachronic Nature of Straightedge Boundaries

The straightedge case suggests that the boundaries of contemporary youth subcultures are in a state of constant flux and transition. We see that straightedge emerged largely out of the American punk rock scene of the late 1970s and early 1980s, when Ian MacKaye mobilized the latent sentiments of punks discontented with the subculture's nihilistic emphasis on drinking, drugs, and casual sex. Opposition to such lifestyle practices defined the boundaries of the straightedge subculture for at least several years and remains a dominant aspect of its ideology twenty-five years later. By the mid-1980s and into the 1990s, however, straightedge had endured several significant transitions and even schisms in its subcultural boundaries, notably an emerging emphasis on vegetarianism and animal rights in the mid-1980s, the appearance of ultramilitant hardline factions in the late 1980s, and the trend to convert to Krishna Consciousness during the early 1990s.

Straightedge is clearly a phenomenon not easily restricted within readily identifiable cultural boundaries. Such boundaries may seem both identifiable and relatively stable when we view a cross-section of the subculture over a small range in time. When we view the subculture as a whole and in historical context, however, these boundaries blur and shift; it soon becomes apparent that they are less sharp and far more subject to change than they first appear.

## The Complexity of Straightedge Identity

Not only the boundaries of straightedge culture but also its membership is complex. This is clearly illustrated through comparisons of various individuals' motivations for transitioning into a straightedge identity. Many straightedgers apparently form their identities in reaction to a former lifestyle that they have now rejected. Some straightedgers explained how they had been heavily involved with alcohol and other drugs before claiming a straightedge identity. For them, straightedge is both a path to a healthier life and a means of achieving goals that otherwise would be unattainable. Other straightedgers, however, did not describe a history of alcohol and drug use. On the contrary, these individuals explained that they had been living a straightedge-compatible lifestyle all along. For them, straightedge appeared as an identity revelation. Thus, while some people feel that they *became* straightedge, others have a sense that they *always have been* straightedge. Still others claimed a straightedge identity in reaction to problems experienced by people in their primary social networks.

However a straightedge identity is acquired, it usually is not exclusive; most members of the subculture balance their straightedge identity with a plethora of others. Some individuals maintain different subcultural identities— for example, straightedge and skinhead—at the same time. Others maintain important political and religious identities. In some cases, straightedgers report minor conflicts between straightedge and other competing identities. Some female straightedgers explained to me, for example, that straight-edge occasionally does not openly accommodate their identities as women. These alternate or competing identities undoubtedly affect peoples' experiences and understandings of straightedge, which in turn impact their identities as members of the group.

In sum, the straightedge case should alert researchers to the importance of identity salience when discussing subcultural affiliation. Straightedge is not a quality that must be either present or absent in one's identity. On the contrary, the salience of one's straightedge identity is something that emerges, ebbs, flows, disappears, and perhaps even reappears at particular points in an individual's life. Moreover, since each person is affected by his or her subjective life experiences, we see a subculture whose members espouse a seemingly infinite range of variation in what constitutes a legitimate or authentic straightedge identity.

## The Relationship Between Boundary and Identity Transition

While transitions in boundaries and changes in the identities of straightedge individuals are intrinsically interesting, it is important to reiterate that these changes are likely interconnected. Changes in straightedge subcultural boundaries have an impact on individual identities, which in turn act back upon the norms, values, and beliefs that denote the general boundaries of the subculture. Some noteworthy straightedge boundary fluctuations, such as the emergence of schismatic factions, probably stem from microlevel processes of interaction among discontented affiliates. Once new schismatic factions emerge, however, new sets of subcultural boundaries or parameters are created, boundaries that have a coercive effect upon the identities of prospective members. In other words, schismatic factions disseminate novel norms, values, and beliefs to which future members will refer when forming their own straightedge identities.

Thus individuals create and sustain an overarching set of straightedge cultural parameters, but then those socially constructed parameters act back upon the identities of current as well as incoming members of the subculture. In this way, we can envision straightedge as a perpetually evolving phenomenon, with each person forming a straightedge identity in relation to preexisting norms, values, and beliefs that is at least partially unique. In time, however, as the individual expresses or transmits this unique identity (via various culture transmitters), he or she impacts those preexisting norms, values, and beliefs at least in a small way, and occasionally in a very large way.

## Implications for Future Research

While this book offers evidence that the emergence, transformation, and schism of straightedge subcultural boundaries are linked to individuals' identity transitions, it remains to be seen if such a relationship is general to all, or even

# Conclusion

most, subcultural groups. Thus, future researchers might address the generalizability of the processes and relationships observed in the straightedge case by investigating the extent to which they hold true for other subcultural groups.

Straightedge culture is not a synchronic, homogenous entity, and that is why a diverse range of subculture theories can explain or account for particular elements of it. The present study applies aspects of strain, subterranean, interactionist, and Birmingham theories, among others, to explain the dynamics of straightedge culture and the people who identify themselves as members. No single theory, however, can properly predict or explain every aspect of the phenomenon. Thus researchers will benefit greatly from avoiding the trappings and restrictions imposed by individual paradigms and instead adopting a multitheoretical approach.

Earlier studies of contemporary youth subcultures often focused on point-in-time cross-sections taken out of historical context. Moreover, such studies often were guided by theories that inadvertently portrayed subcultures as unchanging entities with rigid and easily identifiable boundaries. To avoid treating subcultures as static and monolithic phenomena, an important first step might involve employing a new vocabulary of shapes that at least has the potential to enable researchers to discuss and model subcultures in a way that accommodates their complex and changing nature.

# Works Cited  Index

# Works Cited

Abernathy, J. 1997. "Release the Fiend." *Victory Megazine.*
Chicago: Victory Records (mail order catalogue).

Andes, Linda. 1998. "Growing up Punk: Meaning and
Commitment Careers In a Contemporary Youth Subculture."
In *Youth Culture: Identity in a Postmodern World,* edited by
Jonathon S. Epstein, 212–31. Oxford: Blackwell Publishers.

Anonymous. n.d. "Fuck straightedge."
http://www.drivenbyboredom.com/keithor/fuck_straight_
edge.htm

Atkinson, Michael. 2003. "The Civilizing of Resistance:
Straightedge Tattooing." *Deviant Behavior* 24, no.
3:197–220.

Bainbridge, William Sims. 1978. *Satan's Power: A Deviant
Psychotherapy Cult.* Los Angeles: Univ. of California Press.

———. 1991. "Social Construction from Within: Satan's Process."
In *The Satanism Scare,* edited by James T. Richardson, Joel
Best, and David G. Bromley, 297–310. New York: Aldine de
Gruyter.

———. 1997. *The Sociology of Religious Movements.* New York:
Routledge.

Barbu, Daniel. 1996. "L'Image Byzantine: Production et usages."
*Annales* 51, no. 1:71–92.

# Works Cited

Baron, Stephen W. 1989. "Resistance and Its Consequences: The Street Culture of Punks." *Youth and Society* 21, no. 2:207–37.

———. 1997. "Canadian Male Street Skinheads: Street Gang or Street Terrorists?" *The Canadian Review of Sociology and Anthropology* 34, no. 2:125–54.

Bennett, Andy. 1999. "Subcultures or Neo-tribes? Rethinking the Relationship Between Youth, Style and Musical Taste." *Sociology* 33, no. 3:519–617.

Bertram, Eva, Morris Blachman, Kenneth Sharpe, and Peter Andreas. 1996. *Drug War Politics: The Price of Denial.* Berkeley, Calif.: Univ. of California Press.

Billingsgate. 1989. "Won't Hang Myself." *Victory: The Early Singles, 1989–1992.* Chicago, Ill.: Victory Records (compact disc).

Bloomington Hardline. 1994. "To Stand for Justice." *Tension Building* 1 (independent magazine).

Bold. 1988a. "Talk is Cheap." *Speak Out.* New Haven, Conn.: Revelation Records (audiocassette).

———. 1988b. "Nailed to the X." *Speak Out.* New Haven, Conn.: Revelation Records (audiocassette).

Brake, Mike. 1993. *Comparative Youth Culture.* New York: Routledge.

Buckley, Bruce. 1996. "Earth Crisis: Desperate Music for Desperate Times." *Syracuse New Times,* November 13. http://www.rway.com/newtimes/111396/cover.htm.

Burn. 1990. "Shall Be Judged." *Burn.* New Haven, Conn.: Revelation Records (compact disc).

Clarke, John, Stuart Hall, Tony Jefferson, and Brian Roberts. 1976. "Subcultures, Cultures and Class." In *Resistance Through Rituals: Youth Subcultures in Post-war Britain,* edited by Stuart Hall and Tony Jefferson. London: Hutchinson and Co.

# Works Cited

Cloward, Richard A., and Lloyd E. Ohlin. 1960. *Delinquency and Opportunity: A Theory Of Delinquent Gangs.* New York: Free Press.

Cohen, Albert K. 1955. *Delinquent Boys: The Subculture of the Gang.* London: Collier MacMillan.

Cohen, Stanley. 1972. *Folk Devils and Moral Panics: The Creation of the Mods and Rockers.* London: MacGibbon & Kee.

Confront. 1993. "Payday." *Payday.* Cleveland: Dark Empire Records (compact disc).

Coplon, Jeff. 1988. "Skinhead Nation." *Rolling Stone,* December 1, 55–65, 94.

Davis, Robert C., and Arthur J. Lurigio. 1996. *Fighting Back: Neighborhood Antidrug Strategies.* Thousand Oaks, Calif.: Sage Publications.

Diehard. 1989. *Looking Out for #1.* Huntington Beach, Calif.: Conversion Records (compact disc).

Dotter, Daniel. 1994. "Rock and Roll is Here to Stray: Youth Subculture, Deviance, and Social Typing in Rock's Early Years." In *Adolescents and Their Music: If It's Too Loud, You're Too Old,* edited by Jonathon S. Epstein. New York: Garland Publishing.

DYS. 1993a. "More Than Fashion." *Fire & Ice/Wolfpack.* Auburndale, Mass.: Taang! Records (compact disc).

———. 1993b. "Brotherhood." *Fire & Ice/Wolfpack.* Auburndale, Mass.: Taang! Records (compact disc).

———. 1993c. "City to City." *Fire & Ice/Wolfpack.* Auburndale, Mass.: Taang! Records (compact disc).

Earth Crisis. 1992a. "Stand By." *All Out War.* Chicago: Victory Records (compact disc).

———. 1992b. "No Allegiance." *All Out War.* Chicago: Victory Records (compact disc).

———. 1992c. *All Out War.* Chicago: Victory Records (compact disc).

# Works Cited

————. 1993a. "Firestorm." *Firestorm.* Chicago: Victory Records (compact disc).

————. 1993b. "Forged in the Flames." *Firestorm.* Chicago: Victory Records (compact disc).

————. 1995a. "The Discipline." *Destroy the Machines.* Chicago: Victory Records (compact disc).

————. 1995b. "The Wrath of Sanity." *Destroy the Machines.* Chicago: Victory Records (compact disc).

————. 1995c. "Fortress." *Destroy the Machines.* Chicago: Victory Records (compact disc).

Elwood, William N. 1994. *Rhetoric in the War on Drugs: The Triumphs and Tragedies of Public Relations.* Westport, Conn.: Praeger.

Erickson, Patricia G. 1992. "Recent Trends in Canadian Drug Policy: The Decline and Resurgence of Prohibitionism." *Daedalus* 121 (Summer): 239–67.

Fine, Gary Alan, and Sherryl Kleinman. 1979. "Rethinking Subculture: An Interactionist Analysis." *American Journal of Sociology* 85, no. 1:1–20.

Fiske, John. 1990. *Introduction to Communication Studies.* New York: Routledge.

Fonarow, Wendy. 1997. "The Spatial Organization of the Indie Music Gig." In *The Subcultures Reader,* edited by Ken Gelder and Sarah Thornton, 360–69. New York: Routledge.

Fox, Kathryn Joan. 1987. "Real Punks and Pretenders: The Social Organization of a Counterculture." *Journal of Contemporary Ethnography* 16, no. 3:344–70.

Goode, Erich. 1990. "The American Drug Panic of the 1980s: Social Construction or Objective Threat?" *The International Journal of the Addictions* 25: 1083–98.

————. 1992. *Collective Behavior.* Toronto: Harcourt Brace.

# Works Cited

Gustafson, James P. 1978. "Schismatic Groups." *Human Relations* 31, no. 2:139–54.

Haenfler, R. 2004. "Rethinking Subcultural Resistance: Core Values of the Straight Edge Movement." *Journal of Contemporary Ethnography,* 33, no. 4:406–36.

Hamm, Mark S. 1993. *American Skinheads: The Criminology and Control of Hate Crime.* Westport, Conn.: Praeger.

Hebdige, Dick. 1979. *Subculture: The Meaning of Style.* New York: Routledge.

Hood-Brown, Marcia R., Robert C. Liebman, and John Sutton. 1991. "Purge and Exit: How Ideology and Organization Determine the Path to Schism in Twentieth Century American Protestant Denominations." Paper presented at the annual meeting of the *American Sociological Association.*

*How's Your Edge.* n.d. Interview with Justin Guavin. http://www.howsyouredge.com/interviews/display.php?interview=guav&page=1

Inside Front. 1994. *Inside front* 5 (privately printed magazine, Atlanta, GA).

Insight. 1990. "End the Cruelty." *Victory: The Early Singles, 1989–1992.* Chicago: Victory Records (compact disc).

Insted. 1988. "United." *Bonds of Friendship.* Fountain Valley, Calif.: Wishingwell Records (compact disc).

———. 1989. "Feel Their Pain." *We'll Make the Difference.* Montreal: Cargo Records (vinyl record).

Integrity. 1989a. "Bringin' It Back." *Den of Iniquity.* Cleveland, Ohio: Dark Empire Records (compact disc).

———. 1989b. "Dead Wrong." *Den of Iniquity.* Cleveland, Ohio: Dark Empire Records (compact disc).

———. 1989c. "In Contrast of Sin." *Den of Iniquity.* Cleveland, Ohio: Dark Empire Records (compact disc).

# Works Cited

———. 1989d. *In Contrast of Sin*. Cleveland, Ohio: Dark Empire Records [vinyl record].

———. 1991a. "Tempest." *Those Who Fear Tomorrow*. Seattle: Overkill Records (compact disc).

———. 1991b. "Dawn of a New Apocalypse." *Those Who Fear Tomorrow*. Seattle: Overkill Records (compact disc).

———. 1996. *Humanity is the Devil*. Chicago: Victory Records (compact disc).

———. 1997a. *Seasons in the Size of Days*. Chicago: Victory Records (compact disc).

———. 1997b. *Taste of Every Sin*. Lakewood, Ohio: Holy Terror Church of Final Judgment (compact disc).

Irwin, Darrell D. 1999. "The Straight Edge Subculture: Examining the Youths' Drug-free Way." *Journal of Drug Issues* 29, no. 2:365–80.

Jensen, Eric L., Jurg Gerber, and Ginna M. Babcock. 1991. "The New War on Drugs: Grass Roots Movement or Political Construction?" *The Journal of Drug Issues* 21, no. 3:651–67.

Judah, J. Stillson. 1974. *Hare Krishna and the Counterculture*. New York: John Wiley & Sons.

Judge. 1988a. "Fed Up!"

———. 1988b. "In My Way." *New York Crew*. New Haven, Conn.: Revelation Records (audiocassette).

———. 1988c. "New York Crew." *New York Crew*. New Haven, Conn.: Revelation Records (audiocassette).

———. 1989a. "Bringin' It Down." *Bringin' It Down*. New Haven, Conn.: Revelation Records (compact disc).

———. 1989b. *Bringin' It Down*. New Haven, Conn.: Revelation Records (compact disc).

Katz, Jack. 1988. *Seductions of Crime: Moral and Sensual Attractions in Doing Evil*. New York: Basic Books.

## Works Cited

Kearney, Mary Celeste. 1998. "Don't Need You:" Rethinking
    Identity Politics and Separatism from a Grrrl Perspective." In
    *Youth Culture: Identity in a Postmodern World,* edited by
    Jonathon S. Epstein, 148–88. Oxford: Blackwell Publishers,
    Ltd.

Kent, Stephen A. 1988. "Slogan Chanters to Mantra Chanters: A
    Mertonian Deviance Analysis of Conversion to Religiously
    Ideological Organizations in the Early 1970s." *Sociological
    Analysis* 49, no. 2:104–18.

———. 1993. "Radical Rhetoric and Mystical Religion in
    America's Late Vietnam Era." *Religion* 23: 45–60.

———. 2001. *From Slogans to Mantras: Social Protest and
    Religious Conversion in the Late Vietnam Era.* Syracuse, N.Y.:
    Syracuse Univ. Press.

Kinsella, Warren. 1994. *Web of Hate: Inside Canada's Far Right
    Network.* Toronto, Canada: HarperCollins.

Kirkpatrick, Lee A. 1993. "Fundamentalism, Christian Orthodoxy,
    and Intrinsic Religious Orientation as Predictors of
    Discriminatory Attitudes." *Journal for the Scientific Study of
    Religion* 32, no. 3:256–68.

Kraska, Peter B. 1993. "Militarizing the Drug War: A Sign of the
    Times." In *Altered States of Mind: Observations of the Drug
    War,* edited by P. B. Kraska. New York: Garland.

Krist, J. 1996. August 22). "White Punks on Hope." *Phoenix New
    Times,* August 22. http://www.phoenixnewtimes.com/1996
    /082296/music1.html.

*Krsna Grrrl Fanzine.* n.d. New York: Equal Visions Records.

Lagatutta, B. 1996. "Rebels with a Cause." *48 Hours,* executive
    producer C. Lasiewicz. Livingston, N.J., *CBS News,* February
    22.

Lahickey, Beth. 1997. *All Ages: Reflections on Straight Edge.*
    Huntington Beach, Calif.: Revelation Books.

# Works Cited

Laing, David. 1997. "Listening to Punk." In *The Subcultures Reader,* edited by Ken Gelder and Sarah Thornton, 406–19. New York: Routledge.

Lavey, Anton S. 1969. *The Satanic Bible.* New York: Avon Books.

Levine, Harold G., and Steven H. Stumpf. 1983. "Statements of Fear through Cultural Symbols: Punk Rock as a Reflective Subculture." *Youth and Society* 14, no. 4:417–35.

Levinson, Arlene. 1997. "In Salt Lake City: Youthful Intolerance Turns Ugly." *Detroit News, December 7.* http://www.detnews.com/1997/nation/9712/07/ 12070057.htm.

Matza, David. 1964. *Delinquency and Drift.* New York: John Wiley and Sons.

———. 1969. *Becoming Deviant.* Englewood Cliffs, N.J.: Prentice-Hall.

McGaw, Dickinson. 1991. "Governing Metaphors: The War on Drugs." *The American Journal of Semiotics* 8, no. 3:53–75.

Mean Season. 1994. "Four circles: Kali." *Grace.* Huntington Beach, Calif.: New Age Records (audiocassette).

Metal Maniacs. 1997. Interview with Dwid. www.geocities.com/ SunsetStrip/Alley/6758/integviews19.html

Minor Threat. 1981a. "Straight-edge." *Minor Threat.* Washington, D.C.: Dischord Records (audiocassette).

———. 1981b. "Out of Step." *Minor Threat.* Washington, D.C.: Dischord Records (audiocassette).

Mitchell, J. Clyde. 1983. "Case and Situation Analysis." *The Sociological Review* 31, no. 2:187–211.

Moore, Jack B. 1993. *Skinheads Shaved for Battle: A Cultural History of American Skinheads.* Bowling Green, Ohio: Bowling Green State Univ. Popular Press.

# Works Cited

108. 1995. "Your [sic] No One No More." *You Deserve Even Worse.* Various Artists. Hanover, Germany: Lost and Found Records (compact disc).

One Life Crew. 1995. "Stra-hate Edge." *Crime ridden Society.* Chicago: Victory Records (compact disc).

Porcell. n.d. "Has the Edge Gone Dull?" *War on Illusion* 1: 16–17. [Independently printed magazine available from Equal Vision Records, New York].

Prabhupada, Bhaktivedanta S. 1993. *The Nectar of Instruction.* Los Angeles: The Bhaktivedanta Book Trust.

The Process. n.d. *Satan on War.* Pamphlet. http://www.abrupt.org/LOGOS/sow/sow1.html.

Raid. 1990a. "Words of War." *Hands Off the Animals.* Chicago: Victory Records (compact disc).

———. 1990b. "Cultured Sadism." *Hands Off the Animals.* Chicago: Victory Records (compact disc).

———. 1990c. "Unsilent Minority." *Hands Off the Animals.* Chicago: Victory Records (compact disc).

———. 1990d. "Unleashed." *Hands Off the Animals.* Chicago: Victory Records (compact disc).

———. 1991a. "Your Warning." *Hands Off the Animals.* Chicago: Victory Records (compact disc).

———. 1991b. "Under the Ax." *Hands Off the Animals.* Chicago: Victory Records (compact disc).

Ridgeway, James. 1990. *Blood in the Face: The Ku Klux Klan, Aryan Nations, Nazi Skinheads, and the Rise of a New White Culture.* New York: Thunder's Mouth Press.

Ringworm. 1993a. "13 Knots." *The Promise.* Bellingham, Wash.: Incision Records (compact disc).

———. 1993b. "Necropolis." *The Promise.* Bellingham, Wash.: Incision Records (compact disc).

Rochford, E. Burke, Jr. 1982. "Recruitment Strategies, Ideology,

and Organization in the Hare Krishna Movement." *Social
Problems* 29, no. 4:399–410.

———. 1983. "Recruitment Strategies, Ideology, and
Organization in the Hare Krishna Movement." In *Of Gods
and Men: New Religious Movements in the West,* edited by
Eileen Barker, 283–302. Macon, Ga.: Mercer Univ. Press.

———. 1985. *Hare Krishna in America.* New Brunswick, N.J.:
Rutgers Univ. Press.

Savage, Jon. n.d. *DIY Anarchy in the UK: UK Punk 1
(1976–1977).* Rhino Records (compact disc).

7Seconds. 1984. "Not Just Boys Fun." *The Crew.* Los Angeles,
Calif.: Better Youth Organization (vinyl record).

Shelter. 1990. "Enough." *Perfection of Desire.* New Haven,
Conn.: Revelation Records (compact disc).

———. 1992a. "Quest for Certainty." *Quest for Certainty.* New
York: Equal Vision Records(compact disc).

———. 1992b. *Quest for Certainty.* New York: Equal Vision
Records (compact disc).

———. 1993. "Progressive Man." *Attaining the Supreme.* New
York: Equal Vision Records (compact disc).

———. 1997. "Helpless." *Beyond Planet Earth.* Toronto: Attic
Records (compact disc).

Singh, Chitralekha, and Prem Nath. 1995. *Hindu goddesses.* New
Delhi: Crest Publishing House.

Six Feet Deep. 1994. *Struggle.* Nashville, Tenn.: REX Music
(compact disc).

Slapshot. n.d. "In Your Face." *Step On It.* Auburndale, Mass.:
Taang! Records (audiocassette).

Small, Adam, and Peter Stuart. 1983. *Another State of Mind.* VHS.
Laguna Beach, Ca.: Time Bomb Filmworks.

Snow, David A., and Richard Machalek. 1984. "The Sociology of
Conversion." *Annual Review of Sociology* 10:167–90.

Snow, David A., Louis A. Zurcher, Jr., and Sheldon Eckland-

# Works Cited

Olson. 1980. "Social Networks and Social Movements: A Microstructural Approach to Differential Recruitment." *American Sociological Review* 45: 787–801.

Stake, Robert E. 1994. "Case Studies." In *Handbook of Qualitative Research,* edited by N. K. Denzin and Y. S. Lincoln. London: Sage.

Staley, Sam. 1992. *Drug Policy and the Decline of American Cities.* New Brunswick, N.J.: Transaction Publishers.

Stark, Rodney, and William Sims Bainbridge. 1985. *The Future of Religion: Secularization, Revival and Cult Formation.* Los Angeles: Univ. of California Press.

———. 1987. *A Theory of Religion.* New York: Peter Lang.

Starke, Frederick A. and Bruno Dyck. 1996. "Upheavals in Congregations: The Causes and Outcomes of Splits." *Review of Religious Research* 38, no. 2: 159–74.

Stoecker, Randy. 1991. "Evaluating and Rethinking the Case Study." *The Sociological Review* 39, no. 1:88–112.

Suall, Irwin, and David Lowe. 1988. "Shaved for Battle: Skinheads Target America's Youth." *Political Communication and Persuasion* 5, no. 2:139–44.

Sykes, Gresham M., and David Matza. 1957. "Techniques of Neutralization: A Theory of Delinquency." *American Sociological Review* 22, no. 6: 640–70.

*Terrorizer Magazine.* 1997. Interview with Dwid. [Internet] www.geocities.com/SunsetStrip/Alley/6758/integviews14.html

Uniform Choice. 1985. "Straight and Alert. *Screaming for Change.* Fountain Valley, Calif.: Wishingwell Records (vinyl record).

*Value of Strength #4.* (n.d.). Interview with Karl Buechner. http://members.tripod.com/~core4life/ecint.html#VALUE%20OF%20STRENGTH

Varner, Lynne K. 1995. "The Straight Edge." *Seattle Times,* August

# Works Cited

25. http://studwww.rug.ac.be/~jdschepp/sxe/texts/seattle.htm.

Victory Records. 1996. *Strife: One Truth Live.* VHS. Chicago: Victory Records.

Vila, Bryan J. 1993. "Is the War on Drugs an Example of a Runaway Cultural Process?" In *Altered States of Mind: Observations of the Drug War,* edited by P. B. Kraska. New York: Garland.

Wallis, Roy and Steve Bruce. 1982. "Network and Clockwork." *Sociology* 16, no. 1:102–7.

Walser, Robert. 1997. "Eruptions: Heavy Metal Appropriations of Classical Virtuosity." In *The Subcultures Reader,* edited by Ken Gelder and Sarah Thornton, 459–70. New York: Routledge.

*We Shall Fight in the Streets.* 1995. Interview with Dwid. Accessed via Internet, February 11, 1998: www.geocities.com/SunsetStrip/Alley/6758/integviews20.html

Weinstein, Deena. 1991. *Heavy Metal: A Cultural Sociology.* New York: Lexington Books.

Williams, J. Patrick. 2003. "Straightedge Subculture on the Internet: A Case Study of Style-Display Online." *Media International Australia Incorporating Culture and Policy Journal* 107: 61–74.

Williams, J. Patrick, and Heith Copes. 2005. " 'How Edge are You?' Constructing Authentic Identities and Subcultural Boundaries in a Straightedge Internet Forum." *Symbolic Interaction* 28, no. 1:67–89.

Wilson, Brian, and Michael Atkinson. 2005. "Rave and Straightedge, The Virtual and the Real: Exploring Online and Offline Experiences in Canadian Youth Subcultures." *Youth and Society* 36, no. 3:276–311.

Widdicombe, Sue, and Robin Wooffitt. 1990. "Being Versus

# Works Cited

Doing Punk: On Achieving Authenticity as a Member."
*Journal of Language and Social Psychology* 9, no. 4:257–77.

Wisotsky, Steven. 1990. *Beyond the War on Drugs: Overcoming a Failed Public Policy.* Buffalo, N.Y.: Prometheus Books.

Wood, Robert T. 1999a. " "Nailed to the X': A Lyrical History of the Straightedge Youth Subculture." *Journal of Youth Studies* 2, no. 2:133–51.

———. 1999b. "The Indigenous, Nonracist Origins of the American Skinhead Ssubculture." *Youth and Society* 31, no. 2:131–51.

———. 2000. "Threat Transcendence, Ideological Articulation, and Frame of Reference Reconstruction: Preliminary Concepts for a Theory of Subcultural Schism." *Deviant Behavior* 21, no. 1:23–45.

———. 2003. "Straightedge Youth: Observations on the Complexity of Subcultural Identity." *Journal of Youth Studies* 6, no. 1:33–52.

Worlds Collide. n.d. "Effect of the Age." *You Deserve Even Worse.* Hannover, Germany: Lost and Found Records (compact disc).

Yin, Robert K. 1984. *Case study research: Design and methods.* Beverly Hills, Calif.: Sage.

———. 1992. "The Case Method as a Tool for Doing Evaluation." *Current Sociology* 40, no. 1:119–36.

Young, Kevin, and Laura Craig. 1997. "Beyond White Pride: Identity, Meaning and Contradiction in the Canadian Skinhead Subculture." *The Canadian Review of Sociology and Anthropology* 34, no. 2:175–206.

Youth of Today. 1986a. "Thinking Straight." *Break Down the Walls.* New Haven, Conn.: Revelation Records (audiocassette).

# Works Cited

————. 1986b. "Youth of Today." *Break Down the Walls.* New Haven, Conn.: Revelation Records (audiocassette).

————. 1986c. "Stabbed in the Back." *Break Down the Walls.* New Haven, Conn.: Revelation Records (audiocassette).

————. 1988a. "No More." *We're Not in This Alone.* New York: Caroline Records (vinyl record).

————. 1988b. "Together." *Revelation Records, New York Hardcore: The Way It Is.* New Haven, Conn.: Revelation Records (compact disc).

————. 1990. "Modern Love Story." *Youth of Today.* New Haven, Conn.: Revelation Records (compact disc).

————. 1997. "Youth Crew." *Can't Close My Eyes.* Huntington Beach, Calif.: Revelation Records (compact disc).

Zellner, William W. 1995. *Countercultures: A Sociological Analysis.* New York: St. Martin's Press.

# Index

# Index

# Index

# Index

# Index

# Index

# Index

# Index

# Index

# Index